ANUPAMA CHANDRASEKHAR

Anupama Chandrasekhar is a playw̄   ⌂ᴜᴇʀ journalist
based in Chennai, India. She was the National Theatre's first
international playwright-in-residence and a Charles Wallace
India Trust Writing Fellow at the University of Chichester. Her
plays have been translated into several languages and staged at
leading venues in India, Europe and the US. Among her works
are *Free Outgoing* and *Disconnect*, both of which premiered at
the Royal Court Theatre in London. She was a runner-up for the
London Evening Standard Award for Most Promising
Playwright and a finalist for the Whiting Award (UK), and the
Susan Smith Blackburn Prize (US) for *Free Outgoing*. Her
screenplay adaptation of the play was a finalist for the Sundance
International Screenwriters' Lab, Utah. Her short story *The
Wings Of Vedanthangal* was the Asian winner of the
Commonwealth Short Story Competition. Her other plays
include *The Snow Queen* (Unicorn Theatre/Trestle Theatre/UK
and India tour); *Acid* (QTP, Mumbai/Madras Players, Chennai)
and *Closer Apart* (Theatre Nisha, Chennai). Short plays include
Kabaddi-Kabaddi (Royal Court Theatre – International Human
Rights Watch Film Festival); *Whiteout* (Royal Court Theatre,
BBC Radio World Drama) and *Anytime, Anywhere* (Theatre
Kimaayaa)

Other Titles in this Series

Mike Bartlett
ALBION
BULL
GAME
AN INTERVENTION
KING CHARLES III
SNOWFLAKE
VASSA *after* Gorky
WILD

Jez Butterworth
THE FERRYMAN
JERUSALEM
JEZ BUTTERWORTH PLAYS: ONE
JEZ BUTTERWORTH PLAYS: TWO
MOJO
THE NIGHT HERON
PARLOUR SONG
THE RIVER
THE WINTERLING

Anupama Chandrasekhar
DISCONNECT
FREE OUTGOING

Caryl Churchill
BLUE HEART
CHURCHILL PLAYS: THREE
CHURCHILL PLAYS: FOUR
CHURCHILL PLAYS: FIVE
CHURCHILL: SHORTS
CLOUD NINE
DING DONG THE WICKED
A DREAM PLAY *after* Strindberg
DRUNK ENOUGH TO SAY
    I LOVE YOU?
ESCAPED ALONE
FAR AWAY
GLASS. KILL. BLUEBEARD'S
    FRIENDS. IMP.
HERE WE GO
HOTEL
ICECREAM
LIGHT SHINING IN
    BUCKINGHAMSHIRE
LOVE AND INFORMATION
MAD FOREST
A NUMBER
PIGS AND DOGS
SEVEN JEWISH CHILDREN
THE SKRIKER
THIS IS A CHAIR
THYESTES *after* Seneca
TRAPS

Fiona Doyle
ABIGAIL
COOLATULLY
DELUGE
THE STRANGE DEATH OF JOHN DOE

Vivienne Franzmann
BODIES
MOGADISHU
PESTS
THE WITNESS

debbie tucker green
BORN BAD
DIRTY BUTTERFLY
EAR FOR EYE
HANG
NUT
A PROFOUNDLY AFFECTIONATE,
    PASSIONATE DEVOTION TO
    SOMEONE (– *NOUN*)
RANDOM
STONING MARY
TRADE & GENERATIONS
TRUTH AND RECONCILIATION

Stacey Gregg
LAGAN
OVERRIDE
PERVE
SCORCH
SHIBBOLETH

Nancy Harris
THE BEACON
NO ROMANCE
OUR NEW GIRL
THE RED SHOES
TWO LADIES

Vicky Jones
THE ONE
TOUCH

Anna Jordan
CHICKEN SHOP
FREAK
POP MUSIC
THE UNRETURNING
WE ANCHOR IN HOPE
YEN

Lucy Kirkwood
BEAUTY AND THE BEAST
    with Katie Mitchell
BLOODY WIMMIN
THE CHILDREN
CHIMERICA
HEDDA *after* Ibsen
IT FELT EMPTY WHEN THE
    HEART WENT AT FIRST BUT
    IT IS ALRIGHT NOW
LUCY KIRKWOOD PLAYS: ONE
NSFW
TINDERBOX

Frances Poet
ADAM
FIBRES
GUT

Stef Smith
ENOUGH
GIRL IN THE MACHINE
HUMAN ANIMALS
NORA : A DOLL'S HOUSE *after* Ibsen
REMOTE
SWALLOW

Phoebe Waller-Bridge
FLEABAG

Anupama Chandrasekhar

WHEN THE CROWS VISIT

NICK HERN BOOKS

London

www.nickhernbooks.co.uk

A Nick Hern Book

When the Crows Visit first published as a paperback original in Great Britain in 2019 by Nick Hern Books Limited, The Glasshouse, 49a Goldhawk Road, London W12 8QP

When the Crows Visit copyright © 2019 Anupama Chandrasekhar

Anupama Chandrasekhar has asserted her right to be identified as the author of this work

Cover photography: Simon Annand; artwork: Feast

Designed and typeset by Nick Hern Books, London
Printed in Great Britain by Mimeo Ltd, Huntingdon, Cambridgeshire PE29 6XX

A CIP catalogue record for this book is available from the British Library

ISBN   978 1 84842 884 3

CAUTION   All rights whatsoever in this play are strictly reserved. Requests to reproduce the text in whole or in part should be addressed to the publisher.

Amateur Performing Rights   Applications for performance, including readings and excerpts, by amateurs in the English language throughout the world should be addressed to the Performing Rights Manager, Nick Hern Books, The Glasshouse, 49a Goldhawk Road, London W12 8QP, *tel* +44 (0)20 8749 4953, *email* rights@nickhernbooks.co.uk, except as follows:

New Zealand: Play Bureau, PO Box 9013, St Clair, Dunedin 9047, *tel* (3) 455 9959, *email* info@playbureau.com

USA and Canada: Casarotto Ramsay and Associates Ltd, see details below

Professional Performing Rights   Applications for performance by professionals in any medium and in any language throughout the world should be addressed to Casarotto Ramsay and Associates Ltd, *email* rights@casarotto.co.uk, www.casarotto.co.uk

No performance of any kind may be given unless a licence has been obtained. Applications should be made before rehearsals begin. Publication of this play does not necessarily indicate its availability for amateur performance.

Woodland
CARBON
www.woodlandcarbon.co.uk
NICK HERN BOOKS
Printed on Carbon Captured paper

When the Crows Visit was first performed at Kiln Theatre, London, on 29 October 2019 (previews from 23 October). The cast was as follows:

HEMA	Ayesha Dharker
AKSHAY	Bally Gill
UMA / KAVITA	Mariam Haque
GOPI / INSPECTOR	Asif Khan
RAGINI	Aryana Ramkhalawon
DAVID	Paul G Raymond
JAYA	Soni Razdan

Director	Indhu Rubasingham
Designer	Richard Kent
Lighting Designer	Oliver Fenwick
Composers/Sound Designers	Ben & Max Ringham
Casting Director	Briony Barnett
Shadow Puppetry Design/ Direction	Matt Hutchinson
Assistant Director	Tyrrell Jones
Movement Director	Diane Alison Mitchell
Voice and Dialect Coach	Edda Sharpe

Indhu Rubasingham – my friend, collaborator, sister.
This play is for you.

Thanks to

Amma and Appa for your unstinting love, support and wisdom.

Patti – for all those stories.

The late Elyse Dodgson – for your stubborn faith in me.

Richard Alford and the Charles Wallace India Trust and the wonderful Department of English and Creative Writing at the University of Chichester for giving me space and time to work on an early draft of this play.

The British Council – for your generosity.

K. Latha – for your insight into our many rituals.

Anshumani Ruddra – for allowing me a peek into your gaming and app-ing world.

Nikesh Patel – for introducing me to Goya.

Shireen Sheriff Ismail – for your generous spirit and for those late-night gossips about our family.

Carl Miller, Moushumi Ghosh and Sunanda Ragunathan for your friendship and humour.

Characters

HEMA, *forty-eight-year-old woman*
AKSHAY, *her son, twenty-five years old*
JAYA, *Hema's mother-in-law, seventy years old*
RAGINI, *a nurse, twenty-three years old*
GOPI, *a doctor, sixty years old*
UMA, *Akshay's colleague, twenty-six years old*
DAVID, *Akshay's colleague, twenty-six years old*
INSPECTOR, *forty years old*
KAVITHA, *Hema's sister, forty-four years old*

Some of the characters can be doubled.

Note on Text

A forward slash (/) marks a point of interruption.

Setting

A traditional house in Chennai, India, with large windows and sills, where crows often visit.

A bar in Mumbai.

A flat in Chennai.

A café in Chennai.

Glossary

Aiyyo – exclamation of exasperation
Amma/ma – Mother
Appa – Father
Brahmahastra – mythological weapon
Chi chi – sound of disgust
Da – a younger male
Dai – Hey (with aggression)
Kadavuley! – god!
Kanna – darling
Konjum chumma irukiyaa? – Will you shut up for a moment?
Mami – Auntie
Na – brother, as in 'Gopi *na*'.
Nalla Veley! – Thank God!
Parameshwara – oh God Shiva!
Patti – grandmother
Payasam – sweet dessert
Rakshasan – male demon/monster
Rakshasi – female demon/monster
Shiva shiva! – oh god!
SMS – text message
Veshti – sarong-type traditional garment that Indian men wear

Note on the Music

Jaya's music can be Indian classical or devotional. The music
that is turned on for her in Scene One should be the one to be
used in the final scene. The music that Ragini listens to is Tamil
film songs.

*This text went to press before the end of rehearsals and so may
differ slightly from the play as performed.*

Scene One

Wednesday. JAYA*'s room.* JAYA *is asleep. A crow caws loudly at the windowsill.* JAYA *jerks awake, a bit confused. She remembers something and thrusts her hand under her pillow. Pause. She hears something. She retracts her hand and hastily lies down and closes her eyes, when* RAGINI *enters with folded sheets and places them in the cupboard.*

RAGINI. Patti! Are you awake? Come on! I know you're wide awake. Your eyeballs are moving.

RAGINI *puts on music. A young, rocking number from a recent Tamil film.* RAGINI *exer-dances.*

Oh I love this song. Let's get started! Let's get those muscles limber and supple.

JAYA *turns away from* RAGINI, *covering her ears.*

Come on, old woman. We have to do this. What did the doctor tell you? Every day, without fail, or your legs will shrivel and die.

JAYA. Turn off that racket first!

RAGINI. Maybe this will inspire you?

RAGINI *puts on traditional Indian music instead.*

JAYA. Turn it off.

RAGINI. Come on! Up, up!

Get up, lazy bones. Don't you want to be up and about like before?

JAYA. TURN IT OFF I SAY!

RAGINI. Okay, okay!

RAGINI *turns it off.*

Now shall we begin?

JAYA. I don't feel too good. It hurts. Here. I think it's my heart.

RAGINI (*yells*). Hema ma!

JAYA. What are you doing –

RAGINI. Hema ma? Please can you –

JAYA. *Aiyyo!* Stop! Shh.

RAGINI. Then get up!

JAYA *sits reluctantly with* RAGINI*'s help.*

Every day, every damn day I have to jump through hoops so you don't become a cabbage.

Beat.

Are you wearing your diaper? What did you do with the diaper?

RAGINI *looks under the bed, then goes to the window. The crow flies away. She looks out.*

You've thrown it where every visitor to the house can see?

JAYA. It wasn't me –

RAGINI. Who was it then? Monsters? Ghosts? Crows? Do you poop diamonds that someone would touch your stinky diaper? God! You're higher maintenance than a baby!

RAGINI *tries to force a diaper on* JAYA. JAYA *and* RAGINI *struggle.*

Aiyyo, Amma, will you give me a break? I've loads of work to do still.

JAYA *lets her put on the diaper. Silence.*

JAYA. I am going to die.

RAGINI. Okay.

JAYA. In this room.

RAGINI. That is for the best. Shall we begin?

RAGINI *stretches* JAYA*'s limbs regardless.*

JAYA. Help! Someone! Anyone! I'm being murdered!

RAGINI. What a crybaby you are!

JAYA. I wish that you have nuts and bolts in your hips and knees, I wish that you are poked by little iron pieces all day and night.

RAGINI *is unrelenting. More moans.*

You're a monster, a *rakshasi*. I curse that someone will cut off your breasts and nose and ears like Lord Rama did that *rakshasi*.

RAGINI. That's a horrible thing to say.

JAYA. I wrote your name on the diaper, by the way.

RAGINI. What?

JAYA. With your marker pen. On both sides. And your phone number. Anyone who passes by will see it.

RAGINI *stretches and bends* JAYA*'s limbs with some aggression.*

Aaaa! Bitch! Stop it!

RAGINI *doesn't stop.*

Please stop it!

A man's looking at the diaper. He's noting down your phone – aaaa stupid bitch, that really hurt!

Aaa gentle, please be gentle.

Okay, okay. I'll do what you say, whatever you say…

Pause. RAGINI *waits for the catch.*

…if you dispose of the diaper.

RAGINI *considers the proposition as she continues to stretch* JAYA*'s limbs.*

RAGINI. You'll do the exercises silently –

JAYA. Utterly silently… utterly… obediently.

RAGINI. Swear on your grandson.

> JAYA *hesitates*. RAGINI *stretches* JAYA*'s legs*.

JAYA. Aaa – I swear on my grandson.

> RAGINI *stops the physio and heads towards the door.*

RAGINI. No mischief when I'm gone.

JAYA. What can I do? I'm disabled.

> RAGINI *is unconvinced, but she exits.* JAYA *is about to reach under the pillow again when she hears footsteps.* JAYA *withdraws her hand from under the pillow and reclines nonchalantly.* HEMA *enters.*

I finished my exercises, all of them!

> HEMA *searches for something on the table.*

Does Akshay take the train?

HEMA. What?

JAYA. Yesterday, a young man was pushed off a train in Mumbai. They showed his body on TV. Mumbai is not safe these days. Every day a new crime. Tell Akshay not to take the train.

(*Sighs.*) *Kadavuley*, how long has it been? One full year since I last saw him.

HEMA. You video-chatted just ten days ago –

JAYA. It's not the same. You fly to him whenever you feel like it. What about me? Poor boy, who knows how he is, living all alone in some godforsaken city, with no family, no food, nobody.

HEMA. He is, in fact, doing pretty well there – a raise just last month, good friends. I'd say, he is perfectly happy in Mumbai.

JAYA. You don't know that.

HEMA. Of course I do – I'm his mother!

RAGINI *enters*.

Where were you?

JAYA. She's supposed to take care of me. But how can she when she's off gallivanting doing god-knows-what with god-knows-who?

RAGINI. *Oy*, Patti. Careful. What are you looking for, Amma?

JAYA. It's in the living room, in the usual hiding place, next to the hideous vase. I saw it there at lunch.

HEMA. Did you?

JAYA. Yes. You were SMS-ing someone. Akshay likely.

Pause.

HEMA. I never said what I was looking for.

Beat.

JAYA. What else could it be?

RAGINI. I'll check.

RAGINI *exits. Silence*.

JAYA. It's seven years next month.

HEMA (*yells to* RAGINI, *off*). Did you find it?

RAGINI (*off*). No, Amma.

JAYA. Hema, you've been stubborn long enough. The planets… It's too important this time – You must listen to me –

HEMA. Every damn year we go through this, every year we do nothing and every year we are fine – better than fine, actually, now that he's gone. I'm the merriest widow that ever was.

JAYA. *Shiva shiva*, you don't really mean that.

RAGINI *enters*.

RAGINI. It's not in the kitchen either.

RAGINI *takes her phone out from her bag*.

JAYA. It is in the living room, I'm telling you. Go back there, switch on the light and look properly.

RAGINI *calls on her mobile. Sound of a mobile phone ringing*. RAGINI *and* HEMA *try to trace it*. HEMA *lifts the pillow and finds her mobile*. RAGINI *and* HEMA *turn to look at* JAYA.

(*Pointing to* RAGINI.) That witch must have kept it here when I was asleep.

RAGINI. She is crazy!

HEMA *checks her phone*.

Amma, this old woman is constantly doing some mischief or the other. I've never felt this exhausted working with old people before. I can't continue like this on the pittance of a salary you're giving me.

JAYA. Go then. Who is asking you to stay?

HEMA (*checking her phone*). Good God, Amma! Did you call Akshay… Twenty-seven times in the last hour? Why?

JAYA. You don't give me my own phone. I have the right to speak to my grandson when I wish.

HEMA. You silly old idiot, this, this is why. You keep calling him and disturbing him at important meetings –

JAYA. He said he'd call me back but he forgot to. I had to try again –

HEMA. You are a cosmic nuisance, old woman. (*To* RAGINI.) Has she done her exercises?

JAYA. / Yes

RAGINI. No.

HEMA (*to* JAYA). Do your exercises, walk by yourself without any help and I'll book you a ticket to Mumbai so you can cook for your grandson for the rest of your life.

JAYA. This once, I'm begging you. For the good of the family –

HEMA. Save your breath.

HEMA *exits*.

JAYA (*to* HEMA, *off*). You and your son are forgetting your duties to the dead but the dead don't forget, Hema!

RAGINI. You can't force grown people to do something they don't want, Patti.

JAYA. Then let's just call it a day. I really hurt all over.

RAGINI. Nice try. Shall we begin? You swore on your grandson.

The crow is back on the windowsill. It caws.

JAYA. I did, didn't I?

Scene Two

Wednesday evening. Mumbai. A crowded, noisy bar. DAVID *and* UMA *are bent over iPads/tablets.*

AKSHAY. You are a penguin in a hurry. You have one goal: to get to this castle on top of this hill, asap. Your world is a lot like Mumbai, actually, you know, with speedbumps, potholes, small animals scurrying across the roads. Ice skyscrapers, ice slums. Mumbai, but with ice. 'Think local, play global' – that's always been my motto. (*Laughs.*) So, your journey to the hill is full of danger. You need all the help you can get – fish to replenish your energy, magic wings to make daring jumps. Above all, *Penguin Waddle* is a game of strategy. Can you waddle away from danger and reach the castle alive? Can you survive this hellish ice city and become the Emperor Penguin? You'll have to play to find out.

UMA and DAVID *play.* AKSHAY *watches them tensely.* AKSHAY*'s phone rings. He hunts for it.*

DAVID. Akshay, turn off the goddamn thing.

AKSHAY turns it off.

AKSHAY. Sorry. My mother. Or my grandmother.

UMA. What's in the castle? Why do I need to get there?

AKSHAY. There's some sort of treasure there, obviously.

UMA. Such as?

AKSHAY. Um. Fish?

UMA. I've already eaten all the fish I can along the way. What's my motivation? Why do I need to get to the castle so urgently?

AKSHAY. You're just super-famished? Uma, this is just a game.

UMA. I believe in story arcs.

AKSHAY. Okay. So. Your arc. It's hunger. Because you're hungry you go to extreme lengths to avoid being dead. You want to go to the castle because of its untold riches in the form of unlimited fish. Satisfied?

(*To* DAVID.) Do you remember that one time, we got so darn hungry at midnight? Dave and I, we climbed out of our dorm window in the dead of the night and walked five miles to Murugan's bar for some biryani – and some toddy for him. How old were we then? Twelve? Thirteen? And when we got there, who do we find? Maths Master Mani. He said, 'Hey, you two, don't I know you?' And we took off. How we ran! (*Laughs*.) I've never run so much in my whole life. We got sent to the headmaster's office the next morning. Our fathers were asked to come. God, he was constantly getting me into trouble! (*Laughs*.)

DAVID. The penguin does not waddle.

AKSHAY. We're still working on the movement.

DAVID. Uma. Thoughts?

UMA. I'm going to be completely honest here. This game is just not challenging enough for me –

AKSHAY. Nothing is challenging enough for you.

UMA. David.

DAVID. Go on.

UMA. Basically, as a penguin, I'm just doing boring shit and I get rewarded for doing boring shit.

AKSHAY. Come on. There are five story levels and an infinite mode.

UMA. If we get past game one. David, I don't know if you agree, the market is glutted with games like this and *Penguin Waddle*, to me, seems awfully close to *Roo Ride*.

DAVID. *Roo Ride*?

AKSHAY. Not a / chance.

UMA. It came out some years ago. Kangaroo running after a joey that escaped the pouch. Remember?

DAVID. Yeah yeah.

AKSHAY. Totally different species, totally different graphics – Chalk and cheese, man.

UMA. Oh I see you have an underwater level too. Like *Roo Ride*.

AKSHAY. What do you suggest we have instead? Penguins eating fish in a desert?

DAVID *drinks the last of his vodka*.

Do you want more of that?

AKSHAY *tries to catch an offstage waiter's eye*.

Waiter! Lady! Madam! What do you call a waitress?

DAVID. Akshay –

AKSHAY. Vodka for my friend here! Madam! Hey, you!

DAVID. Forget her for a moment. (*Pause*.) Akshay. I agree with Uma. We can't pitch this shit. You heard KRS. He said, country-specific original content. No derivative stuff.

AKSHAY. Okay. Okay. What if there is real treasure in the castle? Like diamonds not fish –

DAVID. It will still be boring shit that not even your mother would play because the premise itself is fucking shit! I'm meeting KRS on Friday and all we have is a bog full of yesterday's vomit. What do I tell him, huh? That you and your boys worked night and day for weeks to come up with this worthless crap? What the hell were you doing all month?

UMA. Can't you buy some time?

DAVID. No. I'm screwed. What exactly is the problem with *Penguin*?

UMA. No enemies to battle. Unadventurous. Easy. There's nothing new in the castle. Just fucking fish. It's just sort of a kiddies' obstacle race now.

DAVID. Right. (*Pause*.) Can we salvage this if we, say, just give the penguin some old-fashioned enemies. Human explorers, oil rigs, I don't know. We need villains. Reconceive this. Make it pitch-worthy.

UMA. Me? You're asking me?

AKSHAY. I can do this. I can re–

DAVID. No. She heads this. You assist her. Any problem?

Pause.

AKSHAY. No, of course not. You know me. I'm a team player. Happy to work with anyone I'm asked to.

DAVID. Well?

UMA. I can try.

DAVID. It's settled then. (*To* AKSHAY.) You and your boys sit with her, come up with something I can use by Friday –

UMA. Friday –

DAVID. It's non-negotiable. And make the bird waddle.

(*Yells, to offstage*.) Can we have a refill?

DAVID *waves his hands to offstage*.

Fucking happy-hour crowd. Fucking Wednesday.

UMA. Whose brilliant idea was it to come here?

AKSHAY. He was in the mood for Russian vodka.

DAVID. Ukranian.

AKSHAY (*to offstage*). Hello! Somebody? Anybody?

DAVID. This is not going to work. (*Hands* UMA *some cash*.) Uma, please can you get us our drinks?

UMA *hesitates*.

Please?

UMA *exits*.

AKSHAY. Smooth! So that's how a man gets his work done, eh?

DAVID. Akshay, your work has been subpar for the last several months. *Praline Pursuit 2* has exactly fifty-four downloads. *Tech Today* said it was buggy and mundane, 'like watching ants sleep'.

AKSHAY. *Praline Pursuit 1* was a hit.

DAVID. Let's not exaggerate. It did moderately well, but that was three years ago. Three years is a lifetime in this industry. Look, bro, we are not in school any more. This is a fucking job in a highly competitive industry and you have to wake up and pull your weight round here.

Work with Uma. Learn from her.

AKSHAY. Oh, you fancy her!

DAVID. What the –

AKSHAY. Are you sleeping with / her?

DAVID. No, asshole. Fact is, she has a finger on the public pulse better than anyone else in the company. Her *Great Escape* and *Microzombies* have been saving our collective hide the last year. She has coding background and a strong narrative talent. The company needs her more than it needs you or me and she's been here only two years. You need to buck up, bro. It wasn't easy getting you this job, with your qualifications, and I don't want to be in a position where I've got to fire you, because, brother, that's a definite possibility the way you're headed. Do you understand?

AKSHAY. Yes, sir, god almighty, I understand.

DAVID. Man up, Akshay. Start taking responsibility for your own failures. You are a fucking anachronism in a market that's constantly evolving. Always three steps behind. We are not in high school any more. Your parents can't keep rescuing you from the world.

UMA *returns empty-handed.*

UMA. Sorry. The crowd in there was too rowdy.

AKSHAY. Not such a problem-solver then, eh? Shall I speak to the manager?

DAVID. No. Let's just –

AKSHAY (*to offstage*). Hey, lady!

Music starts. Plenty of drums.

UMA. Oh great.

DAVID. You're right. This place was a bad idea.

AKSHAY (*yells to offstage*). Hey – we're ready to place our orders if –

DAVID. Akshay, leave it. There's this new place a few blocks away. Pinky Punjabi Restaurant. I'm in the mood for some chicken.

AKSHAY. I got this.

UMA. Akshay, we can sit here for eternity and still not be served.

AKSHAY. Hey, you!

UMA. She can't hear you.

AKSHAY (*yells*). Hey, you!

Oh she heard. Did she just…? You saw that?

UMA. Yeah, she gave you the finger.

DAVID. Dude, it's okay. Chill.

UMA. Let's just get out of here before I end up with a migraine.

DAVID. Akshay? You coming or what?

Pause.

AKSHAY. Sorry. I'm not hungry. That's my story arc. I'm not hungry so I think I'll just… sit here, be served and then head home. You two lovebirds go ahead.

UMA. What?

AKSHAY. Don't forget the iPads.

Scene Three

Chennai. Thursday. RAGINI *wheels* JAYA *into the living room.* HEMA *is tallying bills.*

JAYA. Get me a glass of water. I'll have my pills now. Here.

RAGINI. *Oy,* Patti. You already had them half an hour ago.

JAYA. No I did not. That's why I'm feeling somewhat. It's my palpitations.

RAGINI. Amma, she'll overdose if she just pops pills like candies.

HEMA. Just give her the pills.

RAGINI. Amma, if something happens, I'll be the one in trouble, not you!

A crow starts crowing shrilly outside the window.

HEMA. Nothing will happen to her. Nothing ever does. She has the constitution of a horse. Or most likely, she spat them out the previous time.

RAGINI. Did you?

JAYA. No.

RAGINI. Such a liar you are!

RAGINI *exits.*

JAYA. What are you doing?

HEMA. The bills don't pay themselves, do they?

JAYA. Life would be easier if Akshay were here, for all of us. You are growing old too, you know – Though you dress like a college-going tomato. Many things take a toll on a person after a certain age. Separation, worry.

HEMA. Why on earth am I going to ask him to abandon all his dreams so he can vegetate in this cursed house?

JAYA. This house is not cursed. It's seen births and celebration and wealth. I was born here, you know?

HEMA. You remind me a hundred times a day.

Crow caws. HEMA *shoos away the crow.*

Shoo! I'll kill you if I see you by this window again, you filthy scavenger! I'm going to buy a dart gun and silence every single one of you!

RAGINI *enters with the pills and water.*

JAYA. I've always loved this room. That was my father's / teakwood chair –

RAGINI. Teakwood chair and that, your mother's rosewood table. Now pop the pills. I've a dozen things still to do.

JAYA. Do you know why the crows go 'kaa kaa'?

RAGINI. Pills in your mouth.

Water.

Swallow.

JAYA *swallows her pill.*

JAYA. Many many years ago, when God Rama and Goddess Sita were in exile in the forest, an evil *rakshasan* happened to pass by. His eyes fell on the beautiful Sita and was instantly smitten –

RAGINI. Everyone knows this story.

JAYA. Not this one. It's a different *rakshasan*. Rama was asleep with his head on her lap. The evil *rakshasan* took the form of a crow and began to harass Sita. He pecked at her between her breasts –

RAGINI. Even a goddess can't escape sexual harassment in this country.

JAYA. *Konjum chumma irukiyaa?* The crow drew blood, but Sita didn't utter a word –

RAGINI. She should have made a racket. I would have made a racket.

JAYA. Her husband, after a hard day's labour, had just gone to sleep, so she didn't want to disturb him. The bird pecked at her again, and again –

RAGINI. If she'd screamed her lungs out the first time, there wouldn't have been a second or a third time.

JAYA. Then, a drop of blood fell on Rama's eye and woke him up –

HEMA. About bloody time!

JAYA. Rama turned livid. He snatched a blade of grass from the ground. The crow laughed in glee. 'Is this your weapon? What can a blade of grass do?' The moment Rama's hand touched the grass, it became an arrow.

RAGINI. He fired the arrow at the crow and the crow was killed.

JAYA. Get me those cushions. What do you know about our rich traditions? Fluff up the cushions. Well, Rama shot the arrow and the crow fled. But no matter where he flew, the arrow followed. The crow was exhausted and scared by now. Finally he went to the forest and begged Rama and Sita's forgiveness. The goddess took pity on the poor bird –

RAGINI. Big mistake.

JAYA. 'Recall your arrow, my lord,' she said.

'This is the Brahmahastra. Once shot, it cannot be recalled.'

'Then punish him,' she said. 'But spare his life.'

RAGINI. See, Hema ma, this is why, this is why crimes keep happening! Because people always let the culprits go!

Pause.

JAYA. What have you been saying to her?

HEMA. Nothing. Don't blame me for her opinions.

RAGINI. So the merciful god diverted the arrow.

JAYA. No. The arrow missed his heart but pierced his eye instead. This is why the crows are to date blind in one eye.

HEMA. No, they're not.

JAYA. That's why the crows cock their head this way and that because they've only one eye to see.

RAGINI *and* HEMA *laugh*.

RAGINI. That's the silliest thing I've ever heard.

HEMA. She's sounding more and more like her father these days. He died a year after I married, but at the drop of a hat, he would spout parables designed to prevent young women from going astray.

JAYA. You're missing the point.

HEMA. Which is?

JAYA. Even the gods had to forgive first so they could save the world. Forgiveness is the key.

Pause.

RAGINI. I so did not get that.

RAGINI *exits*.

HEMA. Key to what? Making you feel better? I don't want you to feel better. I want you to feel the full wave of my resentment and anger. I want you to simmer on slow in my ill-will until my bitterness flows through your veins and feeds your guilt.

JAYA. For how much longer? Aren't you tired?

HEMA. Oh I can assure you, I have more stamina than ever for this bearing-a-grudge thing. It's far more entertaining than any game my son may design and I swear it's good for my skin too.

JAYA. Go on, mock all you want! There's a higher power out there that's watching us all and one day, He will act! Mark my words!

HEMA. Oh. Will he open his third eye and burn us into ashes? That's not a bad way to go, if you ask me. So yes, let Him smite me. Please feel free to send Him a special request from me.

AKSHAY *enters*. RAGINI *returns to the room*.

RAGINI. Amma – someone has come in.

JAYA *and* HEMA *spot* AKSHAY.

AKSHAY (*with forced smile*). You're both… fighting still?

HEMA. God! Akshay! What are you doing here?

JAYA (*folds her palms*). Oh *Parameshwara*! My prayers have been answered!

HEMA. You never said you were coming home.

AKSHAY. I, yes, I surprised myself.

JAYA (*to* AKSHAY). You must break a hundred coconuts at the temple tomorrow. I've promised the Lord.

HEMA. You go and break them. Why do you rope my son into all your promises?

And you – why have you switched off your phone? I've been trying you all night yesterday and this morning too.

AKSHAY. Sorry, I didn't realise.

HEMA *hugs* AKSHAY, *who is stiff and awkward*.

HEMA. Look at you. My handsome baby, but you look terrible, like a thug, especially with the stubble – And you've lost weight. No matter, you're here, I'll fatten you up.

JAYA. I'll make him my famous *payasam*.

HEMA. How are you going to stand in front of the stove? You've not been vertical in two years.

JAYA (*re:* RAGINI). She'll help. She doesn't do much in the house anyway. (*To* AKSHAY.) You'd like that, wouldn't you?

AKSHAY. Yes. Of course.

RAGINI. I'll take your bag upstairs.

AKSHAY *hands it to* RAGINI. RAGINI *exits*.

HEMA. What's wrong?

AKSHAY. Nothing. I'll go and have a bath, I must be stinking.

HEMA. Akshay. Look at me.

AKSHAY *doesn't*.

Look at me.

AKSHAY. Ma, come on. I'm fine –

HEMA. Look at me, please.

AKSHAY *looks at* HEMA. *Pause*.

AKSHAY (*pulling his eyelids wide open*). Satisfied? My pupils are fine. See? Not stoned, not drunk. I had just a beer, that's all. Just a goddamn beer. Any problem with that?

Pause.

HEMA. You're probably hungry. I'll fix something quickly.

JAYA. Wait. Where's my hug?

Welcome home, *kanna*. This is where you belong. Don't let anyone tell you otherwise.

AKSHAY (*a bit emotional*). Thank you. May I go now? (*Pause*.) It is good to be home.

AKSHAY *leaves. The two women look on*.

Scene Four

Some hours later that day. HEMA *is reading the newspaper.*
AKSHAY *snatches it away.*

AKSHAY. They say if you read newspapers every day for two
decades your body ages by another decade.

HEMA. That's absolute nonsense!

AKSHAY. Some study somewhere. So mathematically
speaking, that makes you practically a senior citizen.

HEMA. Why, half an hour ago you said I shed a decade since
we hired a nurse for Patti.

AKSHAY. I suppose, mathematically speaking, it all averages
out and you are exactly… your age.

HEMA *(laughs)*. Go on you, puppy. Do your thing, go hang out
with your friends.

AKSHAY. I am hanging out with my friend.

HEMA *(laughs)*. Okay, give me back my paper.

AKSHAY. No.

    AKSHAY *crumples it and throws it away.*

HEMA. What did you do that for? I've not finished today's
sudoku.

    AKSHAY *shrugs.*

    What's with you today? No TV, no paper –

AKSHAY. You'll live longer and thank me for it.

HEMA. What will I do with my time? I'm done with the chores.
The old woman is asleep, finally. Ragini has gone to the shop
and –

AKSHAY *has taken* HEMA*'s mobile phone.*

You kidnapped my phone?

AKSHAY. Oh yeah! For all the time you hid my video games so I'd study for my exams?

HEMA. That's different. It was for your own good.

AKSHAY. So is this. Studies say that spending time with one's son is essential for a long and happy life.

HEMA. Studies say.

AKSHAY. Yep. You're still at three thousand seven hundred.

HEMA. Huh?

AKSHAY. That was your score three years ago. You've not played *Praline Pursuit* since level two. Who does that? Everyone plays at least seventy-five levels. Don't you want to know what your son does?

Well?

HEMA. Don't be mad. I don't understand these things. I was born when games meant playing outside and phone calls meant somebody in the family died.

AKSHAY. Excuses add up years too, you know. This is the easiest game in history. Everyone is addicted to it. There's a second one out too. *Praline Pursuit 2*. It's an even bigger hit. Then there's a new one I'm working on.

HEMA *is about to take her phone back but* AKSHAY *holds it at arm's length.*

Do you want to be young or not?

HEMA (*giggling*). I do, I do.

AKSHAY. So you'll play my game every day. Ditch sudoku. Grow young. Don't be an auntie.

HEMA. I'll try.

AKSHAY (*holds the phone higher still*). Not the right answer. Whoever plays *Praline Pursuit* for ten minutes a day has improved mental acuity.

HEMA. Studies say?

AKSHAY. No, I say.

HEMA *laughs*.

HEMA. I have missed this.

AKSHAY. Me too. I don't know why I left home in the first place.

HEMA. Now you say this. Then a week later you'll say, the house is like a museum, it's haunted by ghosts, I want to get out.

Yet another game between them.

AKSHAY. No, that's what you say!

HEMA. You said it the last trip!

AKSHAY. Did I? It doesn't feel like a museum any more The old things are gone now. The old smells are gone. It feels like home.

HEMA. It's an old-age home. Don't live here. Go to a young city, grow and be wild. Find a girlfriend. (*Beat.*) Do you have a girlfriend?

AKSHAY. No.

HEMA. Is there someone –

AKSHAY (*snaps*). No, ma! For God's sakes –

HEMA. Okay, okay. You know I'll support you whatever you choose.

A small dog yaps. GOPI *appears outside their window. He taps.*

AKSHAY. Doctor uncle!

GOPI. Sorry to disturb – Oh, Akshay is home, is it?

HEMA. Gopi *na*. Come on in.

GOPI (*to dog*). Sit, Caesar! No, sit. Sit. (*Pause*.) There's a good boy.

HEMA *opens the door.* GOPI *enters*.

I WhatsApped you everything but I didn't get two tick marks for hours. So I came to tell you in person.

HEMA. Tell me what?

GOPI. Check it.

HEMA *takes the phone from* AKSHAY.

AKSHAY. Sorry, I put it on flight mode.

Beat.

HEMA. Turn it back on.

AKSHAY *does so. Pings of messages*.

'Ask your mother-in-law to stop feeding those stupid crows.'

GOPI. I saw her do it a while ago. Caught her in the act. Check the picture. (*As* HEMA *checks*.) They eat at her windowsill and then do their nasty on my new car. It's ruined. One million rupees that car cost me. Chevrolet. Glossy red. Now howmuchever I clean, the stains are not going. On the bonnet, on the tail, on the top, stains everywhere. Brand-new car. I'm very upset.

JAYA (*off*). Hema! Who are you talking to?

GOPI (*yells*). Who do you think?

JAYA (*off*). What does he want?

HEMA (*yells*). Will you shut up, Amma?

GOPI. Your family and mine have been friends for decades, since his father grew his first hairs on his chin. At least for the sake of our friendship, do something!

HEMA. They're birds, we have no control over their actions.

GOPI. You have control over hers. Don't feed them, is all I'm saying. Tell that old woman strictly.

JAYA (*off*). Tell that buffoon, I'll do whatever I want in my house! Who is he to tell me what to do?

GOPI. Can she hear us?

HEMA. Oh she has planted ears everywhere.

GOPI (*yells*). I'll sue you! I'll cut off the damn neem tree!

JAYA enters in her wheelchair.

JAYA. It's my tree, my son planted it!

GOPI. It's not on your property. It's on public land! I'm public!

JAYA. You touch it, I'll die and haunt you for the rest of your life!

The mobile phone rings. HEMA *declines the call.*

GOPI. I take care of you, I took care of your son, old woman, when he was dying and in pain. You curse me? Me? Next check-up, I'll stop prescribing you painkillers. In fact, find yourselves another doctor.

HEMA. Oh God, don't say that –

JAYA. Oho! Let him go. Doctors are a dime a / dozen now.

Phone rings. HEMA *swipes it quiet.*

HEMA (*to* JAYA). Shut up! (*To* GOPI.) Please don't mind her. You know how she is.

JAYA (*to* HEMA). Who are you to apologise for me? I will do whatever I want inside this house! You can't stop me!

JAYA exits. The phone rings again. AKSHAY *tries to take the phone but* HEMA *has already answered.*

HEMA (*into phone*). Hello. This is she… who is calling?… David! How are you?

He's…

AKSHAY *shakes his head.*

…not here.

GOPI *is interested.* HEMA *catches him watching her. She turns away and continues the conversation in low tones.*

AKSHAY (*whispers*). That's just – that's my office. I'm supposed to be on vacation and they want me to work from home.

GOPI. Your father used to do that too.

How is Mumbai?

AKSHAY. Full-on. Commute takes hours.

GOPI. Too much crime is happening there. Why, a day ago, a woman was raped by a mob of no-good drunken loafers on a deserted street. It's like something is snapping inside people. Be very careful. Cities are getting very dangerous.

HEMA (*into phone*). I too have been trying all night –

GOPI. Akshay, come closer. It's difficult to have a conversation in this angle. Your father was a great man. Excellent business acumen. He told me where to put my money. He ruled this house like a king. Everything ran like clockwork. Look at the house now. You must take charge, boy. Especially where that old woman is concerned.

HEMA (*into phone*). What do you mean?

GOPI. Look at me when I'm talking to you, young man! Give an elder due respect, I say!

AKSHAY. Sorry.

GOPI. Why do you youngsters have the attention span of a fruitfly? I could listen to my elders for hours when I was your age.

HEMA (*into phone*). Yes, David, I got it. I may be middle-aged but I think I can relay a simple message without a problem. Bye.

GOPI. Everything okay?

HEMA. Yes.

I can only try to convince Amma. She never listens to anyone.

GOPI. What? Oh yes! I'm at the end of my tether, Hema. Next time, I'll take drastic action. (*To* AKSHAY.) Remember what I said. Be your father's son, I say.

GOPI *exits. Pause.* GOPI *returns.*

You should do the opposite of *Angry Birds*. Like, *Angry Car Owners* who shoot at nuisance birds and kill them all off.

GOPI *exits.*

(*Off.*) Come, Caesar!

Silence.

AKSHAY. What did he say?

HEMA. He said you didn't turn up at work today. He said he'd been trying to reach you. He wanted you to call him. He said it was urgent.

AKSHAY *nods, keeps nodding.*

AKSHAY. Anything else?

HEMA. That's it. Why didn't you tell him you were taking leave?

AKSHAY. I wasn't thinking straight. I was a mess. I had to come home. I think I've screwed up.

HEMA. Nonsense! You're a hard-working employee. He can see that. He'd not call you otherwise, would he?

Pause.

AKSHAY. I've really f–

This time, it's…

I can't go back after this. I've…

There are so many of us now fighting for so few positions. Only the best survive.

HEMA. Which you are.

Right?

Right?

AKSHAY. No, ma.

HEMA. That's not the right answer. Are you the best?

AKSHAY. No, ma.

AKSHAY *hugs* HEMA.

HEMA. Studies say you're the best game-writer in the whole country. Let's give it a week. When the dust settles, I'll pay a visit to Josephine and Thomas. I'll give them a very expensive gift. They'll talk to David. It'll be alright, you'll see. Trust your mother. I'll set it right. I'll take care of this.

AKSHAY *tries hard to contain himself. In* JAYA*'s room, a single black feather falls on her white pillow.* JAYA *picks it up and stares at it.*

Scene Five

HEMA *and* AKSHAY *are in the living room.* RAGINI *pushes* JAYA *in her wheelchair.* AKSHAY *is eating.*

RAGINI (*aside, to* HEMA). Amma, can you give her a sedative? She keeps me up all night. She may not need sleep, but I do.

JAYA. I don't have very much time left in this world. I don't want to spend it sleeping.

HEMA (*to* RAGINI). Go to bed. I'll take it from here.

JAYA. Are you done already? Hema, you've not fed him properly.

AKSHAY *makes a face.*

RAGINI (*laughs*). This used to happen in my house too, all the time. With my older brother it was always, do you want to eat this, do you want to drink that, as if he wasn't old enough to make eating decisions by himself. With me, no such thing. They sent me off to work when I was thirteen. I was never a child. He, on the other hand, was always a boy.

AKSHAY *laughs as he washes up at the sink.*

JAYA. When you turn, when you smile, you look so much like Jagan.

HEMA. Nonsense. Everyone says it's me he takes after. Check my Facebook if you don't believe me.

JAYA. Ask that girl. Hey, you! What do you think?

RAGINI *pauses as she's heading out.*

RAGINI. There is some resemblance with the picture by Patti's bed.

JAYA. There!

RAGINI. And there's some resemblance with Hema ma too. Fifty-fifty, I'd say. Goodnight!

RAGINI *exits. Silence.*

HEMA. Well?

JAYA. It's my grandson I wish to speak to.

HEMA. Akshay and I have no secrets.

JAYA (*to* AKSHAY). I found this on my pillow.

AKSHAY. A crow's feather?

HEMA *starts to clear the table.*

JAYA (*to* AKSHAY). A crow has been coming to my window every afternoon for the last few weeks now and cawing his heart out, the poor soul. I am certain the crow was relaying a message to me.

From your father.

AKSHAY. What?

JAYA. Yes.

HEMA. In all our years together, he never strung more than four words at a time, but somehow this crow is always *yak yak yak*!

JAYA. The message was not just from your father. It's from your grandfather and your great-grandfather. Three generations of the dead who are in the limbo realm between Heaven and Earth.

AKSHAY. What do they want?

JAYA. They don't want to be forgotten.

HEMA. We have not. No matter how hard we try.

AKSHAY. The crow comes to you because you've been feeding him. He caws because he wants to be fed. There's no need to attribute paranormal reasons to biological acts.

JAYA. Your father – he never once missed the ritual of honouring his father and forefathers, not once in twenty-five years. Look where it got him! Everything he touched was gold. Everyone used to say, he was the gods' favourite. We flourished. Jagan insisted on the ceremony even when he was sick and in his deathbed. You remember that, Hema? How thin he was and how much he was wheezing in the smoke during the ceremony! Still he was so devout.

AKSHAY. And still he died.

JAYA. Peacefully.

AKSHAY. Yes he did. The bastard.

JAYA. Language! This is what you've taught your son?

HEMA. No matter what Jagan did, who he hurt, he escaped its consequence. Therefore, there is no god or justice. This is what you have taught my son.

RAGINI *returns*.

RAGINI. Sorry, Amma. (*To* JAYA.) Where is my phone?

AKSHAY *begins to search but* RAGINI *stares at* JAYA.

HEMA. Amma?

JAYA *hands* RAGINI *her phone*.

RAGINI. You've called someone.

HEMA. Who?

Whose number is that?

RAGINI. You used up twenty-two rupees! I have only three rupees' balance.

Look, Amma, this is harassment! I can't make a call now, I can't send a text. I am practically a prisoner here!

HEMA. Don't be melodramatic. I'll pay you back tomorrow. We'll sort it all out after a good night's sleep.

RAGINI. I'm warning you, Amma! One more trick like this, I'm leaving!

RAGINI *leaves*.

AKSHAY. I am here, so who did you call?

JAYA. Whatever I do, I do for the whole family.

AKSHAY. Who?

JAYA. The fortnight to worship our dead is next month.

AKSHAY. I don't care if he's in Hell or in some limbo world where his soul is tortured or if he finds release and is reborn as a rat. As far as I'm concerned he's gone. That chapter is closed. You know what my answer is, what it's always been.

AKSHAY exits. HEMA pushes the wheelchair towards JAYA.

HEMA. You have to help me. I'm not going to lift you on my own.

JAYA. I know you think I'm your enemy. I know at one point, I was. But will you believe me when I say I was just trying to be a good wife and mother? That's all we can be. Try to be good wives and good daughters and good mothers. That's our karma.

HEMA tries to lift JAYA to place her on the wheelchair.

I don't want to go back to my room. I don't want to sit there watching the fan go round and round. I don't want to wait in the dark for the God of Death to appear before me. Sit with me, Hema.

For a few minutes, please.

HEMA sits. JAYA holds HEMA's hand.

HEMA. Was it the priest you called?

Silence.

It's of no use.

JAYA. We'll see.

HEMA. Do you want some music on?

JAYA. No.

HEMA. You used to find it soothing.

JAYA. No. No music.

Silence.

All my life, I've tried very hard to be like the Goddess Sita. A pious wife. But it is so difficult to be someone like that.

HEMA. You used to listen to MS's bhajans. I'll find it for you.

HEMA *gets up.* JAYA *lets go of* HEMA*'s hand.*

JAYA. No. He was constantly giving you gifts. It broke my heart when he gave you this house. It was mine, my father's and then mine. I gave it to my son. And one fine day, he gifts it to you only two years into your marriage.

HEMA. You know perfectly well why he gave it to me.

JAYA. In all these years, I never once heard you cry.

HEMA. What are you talking about?

JAYA. Every marriage has its ups and downs. But you were happy with him. Or I'd have heard you cry. I'd have heard you fight and scream.

HEMA. How could you not have heard?

JAYA. You stayed with him till the end. You were a good wife. You must be a good mother now. There is power to that role. My Jagan did everything I asked of him. You have similar power over Akshay. Tell him to do his duty. His life will turn for the better. (*Pause.*) Please tell your son.

Scene Six

Monday. The living room. A police INSPECTOR *walks in wiping crow shit off his shoulder.*

INSPECTOR. Bloody crows!

Sorry to keep you waiting. Every day I'm on the road, and I still can't predict the traffic. Sometimes I wish I'd just listened to my father and written my bank exams. I'd be in an AC room today, handling money. (*Laughs.*)

AKSHAY. Amma – Don't we have buttermilk? It's scorching hot outside.

HEMA. Of course. Would you like some?

INSPECTOR. Buttermilk goes some way in making conditions ideal, no?

HEMA. Ragini?

RAGINI *is about to leave.*

INSPECTOR. She your servant?

RAGINI. Nurse.

INSPECTOR. Same thing. How long has this girl been working here?

RAGINI. I've not committed any crime.

HEMA. A few months.

INSPECTOR. I saw some elder diapers on the doorway.

HEMA. I'll kill my mother-in-law! Not literally, of course! (*Laughs.*)

INSPECTOR. Are you from here?

HEMA. No.

RAGINI. What am I supposed to have done?

INSPECTOR. What have you done?

RAGINI. Nothing.

INSPECTOR. Then go get me buttermilk. (*Laughs*.)

RAGINI *exits*.

HEMA. How can we help you, inspector sir? What is this regarding?

INSPECTOR. So you're working with Khel Gaming World as – ?

AKSHAY. Senior Game-Writer.

INSPECTOR. And you did not inherit your father's business?

AKSHAY. No.

HEMA. He wanted to forge a different path from his father.

AKSHAY. I don't have a single business bone in my body.

INSPECTOR. You live in Mumbai?

AKSHAY. Yes.

Pause.

INSPECTOR. Madam, I'd like to speak to your son in private.

HEMA. Why?

INSPECTOR. I'm investigating an incident.

AKSHAY. What incident?

HEMA. Did you double-lock your flat before you came? Has he been burgled or something?

INSPECTOR. No –

HEMA. If it's bad news just tell us.

INSPECTOR. Please understand. I could have easily called you all to the station. I could have made you wait in the heat for hours. But I didn't out of respect for your family name. I have hundreds of cases pending that I should attend to. I want to finish this in the shortest possible time, and for all our sakes, please allow me to ask your son a few questions in private. I will come to you after that.

HEMA. All I wish to know is what happened –

AKSHAY. You're stressing unnecessarily, Amma. Go inside. I'm sure I can clear things up for the inspector.

INSPECTOR. Listen to your son. I will tell you in due course. Allow me to do my duty. Or I'll have to call you one by one to the station.

Please close the door behind you.

HEMA *exits*.

Where were you on Wednesday?

AKSHAY. Which Wednesday?

INSPECTOR. Four days ago. The 26th.

Pause.

AKSHAY. I was in my office.

INSPECTOR. The whole day?

AKSHAY. Till six.

INSPECTOR. And then?

AKSHAY. We had a work meeting. David, Uma and I. My colleagues and I often do that, discuss work over dinner.

INSPECTOR. Where did you have this 'work meeting'?

AKSHAY. Some place in Andheri. David took us there.

INSPECTOR. Was it a restaurant?

AKSHAY. I was too focused on my work, I had an important pitch, I didn't pay attention to where we were.

INSPECTOR. Or was it a bar?

AKSHAY. What is this about?

INSPECTOR. Was it a bar?

Pause.

AKSHAY. I think it was.

INSPECTOR. Name of the bar?

AKSHAY. I really don't know.

INSPECTOR. Was it Bar Zee?

AKSHAY. I don't know the name.

INSPECTOR. Your colleagues have said they were at Bar Zee.

AKSHAY. Then that's where we were.

INSPECTOR. How long were you in Bar Zee?

AKSHAY. Surely my colleagues told you that as well.

INSPECTOR. I am asking you.

AKSHAY. I don't know. Till eight.

INSPECTOR. Then?

AKSHAY. I went home.

INSPECTOR. Home Mumbai or home here?

AKSHAY. Home Mumbai. But I wanted to catch a flight that night.

INSPECTOR. To where?

AKSHAY. Home here.

INSPECTOR. Did you?

AKSHAY. Yes.

INSPECTOR. Flight time?

AKSHAY. 10:30 p.m. Air India. I reached here midnight.

INSPECTOR. Do you have the itinerary? The boarding pass? Taxi receipt.

AKSHAY. I'm pretty sure I threw them away when I came. I can probably take a printout –

INSPECTOR. Of course you can. Everybody is tech-savvy these days. Everybody hacks, pirates, fakes.

AKSHAY. I don't. Will you please tell me what this is all about?

INSPECTOR. The bargirl case. You must have heard the news.

AKSHAY. No.

INSPECTOR. Really? A waitress from Bar Zee was… brutalised by a group of men. Because someone propositioned her and she said no. Did you proposition her?

AKSHAY. No! Absolutely no!

INSPECTOR. I think it was you.

AKSHAY. What? You've got to be joking! There is no way it was me!

The INSPECTOR *looks at* AKSHAY *for a few moments and then goes to the door and opens it.* HEMA *has been eavesdropping. She enters with a glass of buttermilk.*

INSPECTOR. Good. I don't have to repeat everything.

HEMA. What exactly is going on?

AKSHAY. He's saying – a girl from a bar was… I – I was at the bar. With other people! I swear to God I didn't do it –

HEMA. Are you accusing my son? How dare you –

INSPECTOR. Calm down, madam. No one is accusing anyone of anything. Yet.

AKSHAY. I am not – the place was crowded, man. There were other men there – completely drunk, rowdy men! You should be following up on them, not me! I am innocent!

INSPECTOR. Whether you are or not, our investigations will soon reveal. For now, we are talking to everyone who was placed in the area at a particular time. (*To* HEMA.) It's routine investigation, madam.

HEMA. Well, inspector, as you can see, he comes from a good family. He would never do anything like that. You're wasting your time here.

INSPECTOR. He seems to have left Mumbai in a hurry.

AKSHAY. Come on! That's got nothing to do with the girl!

HEMA. Let me answer that – He felt overworked and ill. He came home to recover. I see nothing wrong with that. Do you?

Pause.

INSPECTOR. Email me your booking details. Also give me a printout.

AKSHAY. Of course!

INSPECTOR. Now.

AKSHAY. Now? My internet is not working.

INSPECTOR. Of course it wouldn't. Do you want me to check. (*Laughs.*) I've got quite the magic hands. Many things that may not work for you work for me.

HEMA. That won't be necessary. Go have a look, try to fix it.

AKSHAY. Ma –

HEMA. Go, *da*, I'll take care of it.

Pause before AKSHAY *exits.*

She was working in a bar, inspector. What do you expect? She was serving men alcohol. Wearing what? A short dress? What sort of girl works in such a place.

INSPECTOR. No girl deserves what was done to her. When my colleague found her, her face was battered beyond recognition. Her body was cut and mutilated as if some wild animals had a go at her.

HEMA. I am sorry for her. But it has nothing to do with Akshay!

INSPECTOR. Madam. It was a very brutal crime. Read today's papers. Everyone is clamouring for action to be taken.

HEMA. Then pursue the real culprit! Stop harassing us!

INSPECTOR. Madam. I am only following the procedure. See, there's the matter of the semen we found on the girl. We have to take samples from all our suspects. Including your son.

(*Pause*.) I knew it'd get your attention. (*Pause*.) I'd like some buttermilk, please.

HEMA *hands the* INSPECTOR *the glass of buttermilk*.

No, madam. That's not what I mean. (*Pause*.) You understand, don't you? (*Pause*.) Come, madam. You're no stranger to the way the police system works. (*Pause*.) We know he was at the bar the night of the crime. The thing is, everybody wants some names, culprits or no. I've been careful to not bring shame to a good, reputed family. I could have easily leaked this to the press. And then, you and I know, there is no way out.

Pause.

HEMA. How much?

INSPECTOR. Five hundred thousand rupees.

HEMA. What?

INSPECTOR. Think of your son's future. Think of the decades of goodwill the family enjoyed in the society. Do you want all that to be tarnished because you're a little tight-fisted? In return, I may accept whatever 'proof' your son offers. I may not find it necessary to cross-check with the airlines. And I may accept his statements as facts. I may not cross-check this with the neighbours or colleagues. (*Pause*.) I may not leak his name to any journalist. How I act is entirely dependent on you. (*Pause*.) You'll have to decide fast.

RAGINI *enters*.

RAGINI. Amma. She wants to come here.

HEMA. Don't let her.

RAGINI *is about to exit*.

INSPECTOR. Ragini, is it? Come here, girl. You live here, don't you?

RAGINI. Yes, sir.

INSPECTOR. Were you here when the young man came home?

HEMA. She's just a nurse –

INSPECTOR. I'm just doing my duty. Answer me. Look at me.

RAGINI. Yes.

INSPECTOR. When was it?

Pause.

HEMA. You remember we made –

INSPECTOR. Keep quiet, madam. Or I'll book you for interfering with the law.

AKSHAY *enters with a printout. Pause.*

(*To* AKSHAY.) You shut your mouth. (*To* RAGINI.) No, look at me. Don't look at them. Good. Now answer.

Pause.

RAGINI. Wednesday night. I remember because we made idlis.

INSPECTOR. You too had your ears stuck to the door?

RAGINI. No, sir.

INSPECTOR (*to* RAGINI). You can go now.

RAGINI *exits. The* INSPECTOR *takes the printout from* AKSHAY *and studies it.*

(*To* HEMA.) I can easily cross-check this with the airlines, you know? Or have you decided?

HEMA. I have.

INSPECTOR. Good. I'm glad you see it my way. Your husband would have approved. (*Pause.*) Don't worry, madam. Luck is on our side. The girl is in a serious condition but still alive. She'll pull through and in a few weeks people will forget the incident, provided, of course, my colleagues and I don't remind people. If she had died, people would expect heads to roll and I wouldn't have been of much help. I've a helping tendency, that's why I joined the police.

Scene Seven

Two days later. KAVITHA*'s flat.* KAVITHA *is clutching her nightie to her chest. Beat.*

KAVITHA. Come in. But don't breathe. (*Laughs.*) There's dust everywhere! I didn't think anyone would visit today with both Venu and the girls away and you always call before you come and in any case you said you were busy and Akshay was home.

HEMA. I thought Venu would be home today.

KAVITHA. He had to fly to Singapore. I tore my nightie trying to clean this stupid fan. Sit, sit! I'll just stand here like a model, if that's okay with you, because if I sit, it'll start to gape. So will you, actually. (*Laughs.*)

HEMA. Can't you cover up with a towel or something?

KAVITHA. God, what does it matter? We're sisters. We're two old cars with the same body parts.

    KAVITHA *laughs.* HEMA *doesn't.*

    I forget you're a prude. I wasn't expecting anyone, was I, to dress in my silk sarees?

HEMA. Don't you have a safety pin?

    HEMA *gives her a pin.*

KAVITHA. My ever-practical sister! What would I do without you!

    KAVITHA *pins up her bodice.*

HEMA. When will Venu be back?

KAVITHA. In three weeks. He's gone a whole month this time. That's good because I now have all the time in the world to clean and downsize. I've been wanting to do this since the girls outgrew their toddler clothes. (*Laughs*.) Do I pass the Hema Censor Board? You should have had a daughter, Hema. You've become horribly sexist with just one son. (*Laughs*.) Oh go on now, tell me why you're sitting there looking so... doomed.

HEMA. There's nothing really.

KAVITHA. Sisters share secrets. I tell you all of mine, like a pre-teen. But you, you are a miser with them. Is it money, Hema?

HEMA. No.

Silence.

I'll let you clean then.

KAVITHA. Are you leaving?

HEMA. If you can ask Venu to call me –

KAVITHA. I won't.

HEMA. What?

KAVITHA. You seek him out when he's not even your blood relative.

HEMA. I need legal advice.

Pause.

KAVITHA. It's not Akshay, is it?

HEMA. No, of course not. It's not his fault, Kavi.

KAVITHA. What happened, Hema? Is it a girl?

HEMA. What – Why do you automatically assume it's a girl?

KAVITHA. He's at that age –

HEMA. That doesn't mean it has anything to do with a girl. If you'd spent time with Akshay for more than one hour a year, you'd know he's a sensitive respectful boy. It's unfair that you're tarring him with the same brush as his father. He has never had a problem with a girl. I'd worry more about your daughters, Mittu and Kutti, and the short short dresses they wear and the late-night parties they go to, than Akshay.

KAVITHA. My girls are clever, independent women. They are not what they wear. And I just meant maybe Akshay has a girlfriend – Just let's just forget this. It's come out all wrong. Look, I'm hot and tired – it's obviously not my day. Why don't you just tell me what he has done?

HEMA. There you go, jumping to yet another conclusion. What gives you the bloody right to cast aspersions on him? You don't know him.

KAVITHA. It was a harmless / question.

HEMA. For the record, I want legal advice because something was done to him. By his bosses, based on rumours and speculation.

KAVITHA. Okay. So what was done to him?

HEMA. I'll speak only to his lawyer.

Pause.

KAVITHA. Fine. I'll ask Venu to give you a call.

KAVITHA *texts Venu.*

There. Done. Happy?

HEMA. Thank you. I'd better be going. I'll see you later then.

KAVITHA. Now that I've served the purpose. (*Pause.*) I met David's mother yesterday at the club. She was telling me about the bargirl, you know the one –

HEMA. I know.

KAVITHA. Poor David, he's distraught. He knows the girl apparently, he goes to the bar often, he has meetings there.

HEMA. You don't know anything. You're being fed all sorts of rubbish by that silly Josephine.

KAVITHA. She just remarked in passing that David was upset. What's going on?

HEMA. Akshay got fired. David fired my boy just because of some routine police inquiries. And why? Because her boy arranged for a stupid office meeting in a bar. In a bar! Who does that?

KAVITHA. Hence Venu.

HEMA. The police have given Akshay a clean chit. He is innocent and I'll be damned if I let some alcoholic upstart destroy his reputation. I don't care if you believe me or not.

Pause.

KAVITHA. I don't deserve to be treated like this by you. I don't think you understand what it was like for me, to see you beaten to a pulp time and time again.

HEMA. It's an old story / you keep rehashing.

KAVITHA. Is it? – Then why do I still get nightmares about it? It's always the same thing. I keep trying to drive through the city trying to find you when I know he's pounding your bones to powder, I keep looking everywhere, but I never find you. Then I wake up in cold sweat.

Pause.

HEMA. I'm sorry.

KAVITHA. Are you really? I'm just the poor sister who has to drop everything, my life, my family, every time that fucker decided to realign your bones. Every time it was I who had to take you to a doctor who'd ask no questions. I'd have to come back to your place and cook and feed your son and your mother-in-law – the hag who wouldn't say a word to me. Even after Akshay grew up to be a strapping lad, it was still I who had to come running to you because he never did a thing to stop his maniac father.

HEMA. Akshay was scared to death of Jagan –

KAVITHA. All you had to do was leave him, for your own well-being. You never did.

HEMA. How could I, Kavi? I'd have lost my son. No judge would give custody of a child, a male child, to a mother who has no income.

KAVITHA. We would have found you a job –

HEMA. With basic pay. What good was that? He, on the other hand, was a powerful man. He could manipulate the system. I know that better than anyone. No, Kavi, I was better off as wife and mother than as a penniless divorcee with no son.

KAVITHA. Just be grateful you're a widow and not a corpse.

Silence.

Don't be mad at me. I hate it when you leave in the middle of an argument and stop talking to me for weeks. And always I have to make the first move. Why is that?

Pause.

HEMA. You've not pinned your nightie right.

Let me –

KAVITHA (*swatting away* HEMA's *hand*). Go away!

HEMA. I'm not a good sister, am I?

KAVITHA. You're lousy.

KAVITHA *lets* HEMA *repin her nightie.*

In JAYA's *room, another black feather falls. As she looks up, shadows emerge. The room fills with moving shadows.*

Scene Eight

JAYA's room. It's noon, but the curtains are drawn. It's dark.
A shadow of a man. The man is AKSHAY.

JAYA. Is that you, *kanna*?

AKSHAY. Sorry –

JAYA. Why are you standing so far away? Come here.

AKSHAY. Go back to sleep. I'll come back / later.

JAYA. No no no, don't go, don't go. I'm wide awake. Stay with
me. I've been expecting you.

AKSHAY. Have you?

JAYA. Yes. I had a feeling this morning, deep in my bones.
I knew you'd visit me. You always do when you're upset,
since you were a little boy. You know you can tell me
anything.

Silence.

AKSHAY. I… It's such a horrible, mangled mess. I wish I could
stop feeling this, this sick feeling in the pit of my stomach.
There's been no arrest, not one, which makes me very very
afraid.

JAYA. Is it the girl? She is lying.

AKSHAY. She hasn't said anything. She's still unconscious.

JAYA. Then she'll wake up and tell everyone the truth.

Pause.

AKSHAY. Or she may wake up completely mixed up, she may
not recognise the real culprits. I mean, I look ordinary. I look
like any man on the street. What if she wakes up and says
I did it?

JAYA. She won't.

AKSHAY. We don't know that. I don't know what to wish for any more. That she wakes up or that she doesn't.

JAYA. We'll make her tell the truth. We always do.

AKSHAY. What do you mean?

JAYA. You're innocent. She's lying. Your father will take care of everything.

AKSHAY. My father.

JAYA. He'll solve everything. You're just a boy, you have your whole life ahead of you.

   Pause.

AKSHAY. What are you saying?

JAYA. Your father knows people. He knows the police. Don't worry. He'll talk to Gopi's father. Everything will be alright. You'll see.

AKSHAY. Whose father?

JAYA. What?

AKSHAY. You said 'Gopi's father'.

JAYA. Did I?

AKSHAY. Why did you say Gopi's father?

   Pause.

   Who am I?

JAYA. What?

AKSHAY. What is my name?

JAYA. *Kanna*, what's the matter?

AKSHAY. What's my damn name?

JAYA. I don't understand. Why are you angry with me?

AKSHAY. Screw that.

AKSHAY *draws the curtains back, letting in a flood of intense noon light.* JAYA *cringes uncomfortably. She is half-asleep, half-awake.*

Wake up!

JAYA. Aah my eyes! Too bright! Close the curtains!

AKSHAY. Who am I? Look at me, look at me.

AKSHAY *shakes her lightly by the shoulders.* JAYA *wakes up but screws her eyes shut.*

Come on! Who am I?

RAGINI *enters.*

RAGINI. Hey hey. What's going on? What happened?

AKSHAY. She thinks I'm my father.

RAGINI. Who is he, Patti? This man here.

JAYA. Won't tell you.

RAGINI. Why, is it a state secret?

JAYA. Go away, girl. Call your, whoever-it-is-you-call-every-other-minute, and get out of my hair.

RAGINI. Me, she recognises me with her eyes closed.

AKSHAY. Open your eyes.

JAYA. Won't, won't.

RAGINI. Why not?

JAYA. Because if I do, he'll go away.

RAGINI. Who will?

Pause.

Who will go away, Patti?

JAYA. Jagan.

AKSHAY. Shit.

RAGINI. Patti, he's dead. He's been gone seven years.

Pause.

JAYA. I know that.

RAGINI *goes to the side table and looks at the bottle.*

RAGINI. Sleeping pills. Patti! How many did you take?

JAYA *lifts one finger.*

There's a reason why the doctor said you should take it only at night.

JAYA. It is my night. He's a nincompoop.

RAGINI (*to* AKSHAY). Don't look so frightened. She's fine.

RAGINI *adjusts the curtains so it's not too bright, not too dark.*

Open your eyes, old woman.

JAYA. No.

Beat.

RAGINI. Hema ma! We need to call Dr Gopi!

JAYA *pops her eyes open.*

JAYA. No no!

RAGINI (*to* AKSHAY). There you go!

AKSHAY. Who am I?

JAYA. As if I don't know! My brain is not addled though your mother would be happy to believe it. Any excuse to send me off somewhere!

Why are you standing there like a coat stand? Don't you have work to do?

RAGINI. Oi, old woman, careful. Your food is cold. Shall I heat it up for you?

JAYA. Leave my lunch be! Go away, do something more than swish about like a quarter-rupee starlet!

RAGINI. I dream of the day I can quit this job and drop your mouth in the washing machine.

RAGINI *exits. Long silence.*

JAYA. You look so much like him, the build, the face, the eyes –

AKSHAY. For the last time. I am nothing like him.

Crows caw and fly to the sill. JAYA *caws back to them.*

JAYA. Kaa! Kaa!

Kaa! Kaa!

You know what they say. If you feed the crows, you feed your dead kin.

AKSHAY. You think he is starving?

JAYA. Yes. My son will feel hunger. He'll feel sorrow and pain.

AKSHAY. You said my father had problems with some girl –

JAYA. No I didn't.

AKSHAY. What did he do? Have an affair? Did he get some girl pregnant or something?

JAYA. Don't be silly.

AKSHAY. What happened then?

JAYA. Nothing happened.

AKSHAY. You said –

JAYA. You misheard me.

AKSHAY. Why did my grandfather approach / Dr Gopi's father?

JAYA. Kaa kaa! Are you hungry, my darling? (*To* AKSHAY.) *Kanna*, are you going to take the ramblings of an old woman seriously?

Caws of crows.

AKSHAY. Patti, please tell me the truth. Was it… Did he…?

Crows caw, fighting amongst each other for rice morsels.

JAYA. Please can you place some rice on the sill?

AKSHAY. Answer me. Did he ever…?

JAYA (*to crows*). Coming, coming, darling! (*To* AKSHAY.) *Kanna!*

AKSHAY. Did he ever talk to you about… his rage?

JAYA. What rage?

AKSHAY. Did he ask for help?

JAYA. What?

AKSHAY. Did you take him to a psychiatrist?

JAYA. Why would I do that? He was not mad.

AKSHAY. Because he wanted to be saved! Surely he wanted that. Surely he realised he had a monster in his veins that made him go berserk at the slightest provocation.

JAYA. He was not a monster. He was a man of values, a paragon, a successful businessman, a devoted family man, everybody looked up to him. Everybody loved him.

AKSHAY. You are wrong, Patti. Some people shouldn't have been born at all.

More crows join.

Scene Nine

The veranda.

HEMA. David! I didn't know you were in town. Josie hasn't come with you?

DAVID. Mama and Papa have gone to the Velankanni Church to pray for my eternal soul. Is he at home, Auntie? I'd like to speak to him.

HEMA. I don't think that's a good idea.

DAVID. I won't leave without having talked to him. I'll just sit here, at your doorstep until he comes out.

HEMA. David, he doesn't want to see you. After all the hours he put in, he feels betrayed by the company, but mostly by you.

DAVID. The feeling, I assure you, is mutual.

HEMA. Why did you fire him?

DAVID. Auntie, this is a private, official matter. I can't discuss the specifics with you but this I can tell you: He sucked at his job. He fucked up – pardon my language. He didn't attend important meetings, he didn't deliver, as I've explained to him in detail –

HEMA. Through email.

DAVID. Well, I didn't have an option. He doesn't pick up my call. He hasn't picked up my call since Dark Wednesday. Why is that, Auntie?

HEMA. The police came home to ask him questions. Did they ask you too?

DAVID. Yes.

HEMA. Are you aware they've completely cleared Akshay?

Beat.

DAVID. Have they? Good for him.

HEMA. Was that girl, Uma, questioned too? She still has a job, I presume.

DAVID. Auntie, please drop it. He'll get another job – you'll make sure of it. Only this time, please get him a job he's more suited to – I don't know what that is, except it's not video games.

HEMA. It's his passion, just as it's been yours.

DAVID. I love to watch cricket too but that doesn't mean I'm a good cricketer.

HEMA. I know he put in long hours. You can't deny that.

DAVID. He put in hours, he sometimes stayed overnight at the office, but God knows what he did, he probably watched porn, because he had nothing to show at the end of the day.

HEMA. Then why did you give him a raise last month?

DAVID. Sorry?

HEMA. And a promotion last year? You liked his work well enough before. Now, since that Wednesday, you've decided he's a bad worker. I can put two and two together.

DAVID. And what have you concluded?

HEMA. That you are jealous of his success and want to eliminate the competition.

Beat, then DAVID *laughs as* AKSHAY *enters.*

AKSHAY. What are you doing here? (*To* HEMA.) Why did you let him in?

DAVID. Your mother wants to know why you were fired when you got a raise and a promotion. She doesn't buy my explanation.

Beat.

AKSHAY. Have you been begging for my job back?

HEMA. Of course not –

AKSHAY. I don't want to work where I'm not respected.

DAVID. Respect? Fucking bastard, I gave you so many chances, I keep giving you chances but you – He was never given a raise or a promotion, Auntie.

AKSHAY. Have you been drinking? You visit us smelling like a toddy factory?

DAVID. The girl is still in a coma.

HEMA. The bargirl?

DAVID. Don't fucking call her that! –

HEMA. David, mind your language in my house.

DAVID. She has a name. I'm not supposed to reveal it, and no one is supposed to use it. She has a beautiful name. She has a family. She was saving up for college. Now, she's in the ICU. I don't think she'll ever come out of it.

HEMA. I thought she was recovering.

AKSHAY (*to* HEMA). Ma, let me have a word with him / alone –

DAVID. No, don't go, Auntie. (*To* AKSHAY.) Don't you want to know what happened after you left? After Uma and I had dinner? I went back to the bar for a drink. I was there till after midnight. I came out at probably quarter past when I heard a weird animal mewl, like a cat caught in barbed wires. The mewl wouldn't stop. I followed the noise, and I saw… in a recess between buildings, the girl and the men. Three men. One was holding her feet, the other her head and arms. One was… he had a broken beer bottle that he was thrusting into her, between her legs.

I screamed, and kept on screaming. I didn't realise until I came to the bar that I had run away. I called the police and gathered all the people I could. We ran to the street, to the girl. She was alone, in a pool of her own blood. Her her her intestines were out. Her face, her face, her beautiful face, bloody and torn and crushed as if someone wanted to erase it, erase it with a broken bottle.

DAVID *begins to weep, but controls himself.*

There were three of them. I've identified two from the pictures the police showed me.

HEMA. And the third?

DAVID. The third… the third, the third… he was the one pressing her head on the ground. I saw him clearly but I was in the shadows. I wonder if he could see me. I wonder if he could identify me. Yeah, the third, he ran away, the fucking coward.

Silence.

HEMA. David, *kanna* –

HEMA *tries to touch* DAVID *but he shrugs her away, violently.*

DAVID. The police didn't show me his picture. I don't know who he is.

If I lay my eyes on him again, I'd ask him: Why?

Silence.

Scene Ten

The veranda. The INSPECTOR *drinks a glass of water. A crow taps against the window.* HEMA *shoos it.*

INSPECTOR. Ragini, is it?

RAGINI. Yes, sir.

INSPECTOR. Have you stayed out of mischief, Ragini?

RAGINI. Yes, sir.

INSPECTOR. You look like you're lying. Why?

RAGINI. I'm not lying!

INSPECTOR. Now you're definitely lying. Are you stealing? Having an affair?

RAGINI. No, sir!

HEMA. Don't you have work to do?

RAGINI. Yes, Amma.

INSPECTOR (*to* RAGINI). Take this glass with you. Where's your son?

HEMA. He's in his room, working. Ragini, will you get him –

INSPECTOR. No, don't. I'm here to speak to you. You can leave, Ragini.

Pause.

RAGINI. If she asks, what should I say?

INSPECTOR. Anything but the truth. Isn't that right, madam? Go now. If I find your ear attached to the door, I'll book you in and chop your ears off.

RAGINI. Every man thinks he's Lord Rama these days.

RAGINI *exits*.

INSPECTOR. The girl has died. (*Silence*.) She was in a lot of pain, so it's probably a good thing. It's not been let out to the media or else the whole country would have erupted by now. We have to make preparations before we do that. We have to come clean about where we are regarding the third assailant.

HEMA. Are you asking for more?

INSPECTOR. Madam, I'm here to do you a good turn.

HEMA. I'm going to call my / lawyer.

INSPECTOR. I don't have that much time. It's been only half an hour since the time of death and already heads are rolling. The superintendent in charge of the investigation has been shunted out. The government is setting up a special committee to investigate. Someone called Sinha is the new chief. I had to tell you, I had to let you know I can't be of help any more.

HEMA *goes to the shelf, takes out an envelope and hands it to the* INSPECTOR.

HEMA. Akshay's phone records. I've highlighted the important bits. They prove he was not in the area during the time of the crime.

INSPECTOR. Where did you get them?

HEMA. Akshay.

Beat. The INSPECTOR *digs into his folder and takes out a sheaf of papers. He hands them over to* HEMA.

INSPECTOR. These are the records available with us. We've been asked by Sinha to procure the phone records of everyone who was known to have been in the area of the crime. We've not submitted Akshay's so far. This one will be of interest to you. It's highlighted too.

HEMA. I don't quite –

INSPECTOR. These are your son's phone records. The real ones. Attested. They place him exactly in the scene of the crime at the time of the crime. Exactly.

Silence. HEMA reads and re-reads the papers.

HEMA. I don't understand.

INSPECTOR. He has been lying to you, madam.

HEMA. It must be a mistake.

INSPECTOR. We have CCTV footage of Akshay with the two accused. It's the moment three strangers meet. One asks another for something, maybe a match. Then the girl walks past. Two men follow her. A few moments later, Akshay does too.

HEMA. It's just CCTV recording, for God's sake! How can you even identify – it's always grainy, and it was the middle of the night –

INSPECTOR. Let me tell you what will happen. The investigators will cross-question the two accused, who will identify Akshay from the photographs we present to them. We now have the phone records and then there's the matter of his DNA samples that Sinha will demand from us. Madam, Akshay's involvement will be conclusively proven and we'll have to take him in for questioning. And it won't be verbal. I guarantee he'll buckle in ten seconds.

Silence.

HEMA. There is no way....

Silence.

People like us do not...

The INSPECTOR *takes the papers from her.*

INSPECTOR. All of them took their turn with her, madam. They practically vivisected her. What kind of family brings up men like them? If it were up to me, I'd clean slice off their manhood. But there is no such provision in our penal code and I am a man of law. You should also be aware. A lot of people are baying for blood. They want the death penalty.

HEMA. Wait, inspector! Would you like something to drink?

INSPECTOR. I can't help you this time.

HEMA. There must be a way, a loophole, something.

INSPECTOR. That's not how the law works.

HEMA. I know how the goddamn law works! Surely there's something you can do. Maybe you could choose to use our records?

INSPECTOR. Madam, there's an eye witness –

HEMA. Who hasn't yet named Akshay. I know who he is and he is a drunkard. His word shouldn't amount to anything.

Pause. Then a decision.

In fact, he's the reason Akshay was in the area in the first place. I find it deeply suspicious. Don't you?

INSPECTOR. What are you implying?

HEMA. Maybe you should get his phone records. You can find out if he was anywhere near the scene of crime.

INSPECTOR. He's a witness. He called the police.

HEMA. How convenient for him. Shouldn't the same yardstick apply to him as to Akshay? Both were there for a meeting. Both are likely to have phone records that allegedly prove they were at the scene at the time of the incident. If my son is a suspect, then so should this witness be. This witness has been in trouble all through school. Anyone can vouch for that. He's an aggressive boy. I think he ticks more boxes than Akshay.

Long silence.

Please may I get you something to drink? All you've had is a glass of water.

INSPECTOR. Madam, are you really willing to scapegoat an innocent?

HEMA. He's the reason my boy was in the bar in the first place. He is guilty.

The INSPECTOR*'s phone pings. He checks it.*

INSPECTOR. They're announcing her death now.

Beat.

HEMA. Inspector?

The INSPECTOR *capitulates.*

INSPECTOR. I'm not saying yes. I'm not saying no.

HEMA. I'll keep the buttermilk ready.

INSPECTOR *exits. Outside the window, crows are lining up one by one and looking inside. Crows squawk noisily.*

Scene Eleven

The veranda. Crows squawk. HEMA enters. JAYA is in her wheelchair, looking out into the open. She turns towards the window and listens intently. The birds quieten down a little.

HEMA. Amma. Are you busy?

JAYA. Yes.

HEMA. Doing what?

JAYA. Nothing. But at my age, it takes up all my time.

> HEMA *sits next to* JAYA. HEMA *holds* JAYA*'s hand and studies it.*

> Is someone dead? Is that what this is about? Who died?

HEMA. The girl. Bargirl.

JAYA. *Nalla veley!* I thought one of you, one of ours… You had me scared for a moment.

HEMA. We all are fine, Amma.

JAYA. What's the matter then? So many secrets you think you can't tell a senile old woman, no? You think I'm blind. My eyes are fading it is true, but I think I can see many things clearer than you.

HEMA. What do you see, Amma?

> *Silence.*

> Tell me what you see. Tell me what to do.

> *Pause.*

JAYA. We…

> Our…

AKSHAY *enters.* HEMA *does not acknowledge him.*
RAGINI *enters with three glasses on a tray.*

Did I tell you about the evil king who committed every
possible crime in history? He married a virtuous woman.
On his wedding night, the strangest thing happened. The
king found that he could not touch her, or even get close to
her. Every time he tried to as much as hold her hand, she'd
burn him up.

RAGINI. With desire?

JAYA. *Chi chi* – The moment he touched her, she'd burst into
flames. Well, the months passed with the king desiring his
wife more and more yet unable to… consummate their
marriage.

RAGINI *leaves.*

Finally, in desperation, the couple visit a holy saint who
advises the king to take a dip in the Ganges and atone for his
past deeds. The king enters the river. He recites holy
mantras. All the sins that he's ever committed, all the sins of
his father and his forefathers, lies, lust, rapes, assaults,
tortures, murders, genocides, every single sin comes out of
his body, through the pores of his skin, through his eyes and
ears and nose and mouth, in the form of crows. Thousands
and thousands of crows. Some fly away and some lose their
wings and fall. And when the last sin leaves his body, the
king is finally free. He can at last touch his queen. (*Pause.*)
That's the power of those mantras. People can start with
a clean slate.

HEMA *snatches her hand back and walks out.*

Hema! Everyone deserves a second chance!

(*To* AKSHAY.) Akshay, *kanna.* Do you understand what I'm
saying?

AKSHAY. Yes. Basically hard-core criminals, mass-murderers,
paedophiles, terrorists will be absolved of everything
provided they do this ritual?

JAYA. They'll be pure as a baby. They'll get the chance to set things right. (*Pause*.) Do you hear that? What's going on?

Sound of an electric saw. Crows squawk in alarm.

My tree! My Jagan's tree! *Dai*, Gopi! Stop! There are nests on that tree, moron! Akshay, stop him!

AKSHAY *leaves*.

There are eggs and chicks on the tree!

The sound of a tree falling and crashing to the ground. Crows screech, then quieten down. Deathly silence. RAGINI rushes in.

My tree! My tree! Gopi! *Dai!*

GOPI (*off*). Those birds were dangerous! They attacked Caesar this morning!

JAYA (*to* GOPI, *off*). My beautiful / tree –

GOPI (*off*). They attacked him like drone planes!

JAYA (*to* GOPI, *off*). You could have simply kept him inside till he grew big, nincompoop!

GOPI (*off*). He's a Chihuahua! That's all he can grow.

JAYA (*to* GOPI, *off*). You useless fool! (*To herself*.) My birds, my poor Jagan.

AKSHAY *returns*.

AKSHAY. The eggs are all broken. There's nothing left. I am sorry.

JAYA. You are an utter idiot, Gopinathan! You deserve to die of rheumatism and herpes! You deserve to be haunted by three dozen ghosts for the rest of your life!

RAGINI. Patti, it's okay. We can plant another tree.

AKSHAY. Yes, I'll plant one in our garden this time. No one can touch it.

JAYA. Nothing grows inside, don't you know? Our garden has been barren for decades. We're cursed.

AKSHAY. We'll try. We'll put new soil and manure. Maybe we can plant a mango tree this time.

JAYA. We are doomed... you are doomed. If you don't honour your ancestors, your future, it will be completely destroyed.

JAYA *looks heavenwards*.

Kaa kaa!

Scene Twelve

Night. The living room. AKSHAY *is playing a shooting game on his Xbox. Realistic sounds of pain and death.* HEMA *enters; she studies him. She sits and watches him play silently. Eventually* AKSHAY *notices her.*

AKSHAY. There she is! When everyone else is asleep, she is wide awake! Are you better now?

Long pause.

AKSHAY *feels her forehead.* HEMA *jerks her head away.*

You're being weird.

HEMA. Is it one of yours?

AKSHAY. When are you going to learn about what I do? I work on games for phones, not for Xbox.

AKSHAY *plays.*

HEMA. Is that… blood?

AKSHAY. The more realistic the games are, the more popular they get. I'm one of the beta-testers. It's not yet out in the market and this is one of the most anticipated games ever. It's an honour, you know, to be chosen to test it out.

HEMA. Do you like this game?

AKSHAY. Can't say. I'm only on level four.

HEMA *studies* AKSHAY *as he plays.*

HEMA. Let me also play.

AKSHAY. What?

HEMA. I want to learn what you do. Let me inside your world. I want to know what it feels like to… do all this. Shoot, kill, have this power.

Beat.

AKSHAY. Who are you? What have you done with my mother?

HEMA *doesn't respond*.

Just want to remind you, you can't even shoot a praline.

HEMA. I want to play. Restart.

AKSHAY. O-kay.

HEMA. Why are you changing –

AKSHAY. You won't like *Urban Killing Fields* –

HEMA. I don't want Scrabble – Or cards. Put that bloody game back on!

AKSHAY. Ma, it's not a game for women –

HEMA. I've lived with your father. I can play *Urban* goddamn *Killing Fields*.

AKSHAY *puts* Urban Killing Fields *back on*.

Isn't it a game that I can play with you?

AKSHAY. It is.

HEMA. Then join me. What are the rules?

Beat.

AKSHAY. So. This is urban dystopia. It's anarchy and chaos. The rule of this game is to survive. Everyone is the enemy. Except me. You and I have to team up and kill everyone. Choose your avatar.

HEMA. That one.

AKSHAY *helps* HEMA *choose an avatar*.

AKSHAY. This is how you move forward. Backwards. Left, right. Press to shoot. If you press this and move forward, you can jump or somersault. Let's play.

The game begins.

HEMA. What should I do?

AKSHAY. Kill.

The game progresses.

Shoot, ma!

You can't just run. You have to stop and shoot. Kill!

Kill!

HEMA *kills. It's not easy for her.*

That's better.

Sniper *Mami* from Madras! Way to go!

HEMA *shoots again.*

You're a natural arsonist and murderer.

They play.

HEMA. The girl who died. What was her name?

AKSHAY. I don't know.

HEMA. Why not?

AKSHAY. How many times have you found out the names of people who served you? You see the man hiding behind that pillar?

HEMA. Yes.

AKSHAY. Let's round up on him.

HEMA *and* AKSHAY *shoot. Sound of man dying.*

HEMA. We killed him.

AKSHAY. Yep.

Pause.

HEMA. What were you thinking?

AKSHAY. What?

HEMA. Just now. When we jumped on him.

AKSHAY. I wasn't thinking. Survive at all costs. It's not real, Amma. Nothing is real.

Hey! You just shot me! What the –

HEMA *shoots some more.*

You wounded me.

Ma, run! Shoot!

HEMA *stops playing.* AKSHAY *takes over her stick and plays. Someone kills her avatar. Sound of a man dying.*

You're dead now.

Silence. HEMA *slaps* AKSHAY. *He is stunned. Doesn't say, do anything.* HEMA *hits him over and over.* AKSHAY *overpowers her.*

What the hell is wrong with you?

HEMA. Her name was Manisha.

Silence. AKSHAY *moves away.*

I gave you everything. I sent you to a boarding school so you'd be away from him, so you'd be safe. I came back to the devil so you could have a good life. I let him violate me every night. I bore the brunt of his temper so you could be a man worthy of everyone's respect. I wanted you to be better than your father. I wanted you to be a good man.

Why?

Silence.

Why?

AKSHAY. I don't know why! It's the truth. I felt… angry. Then I lost my head. I only wanted to hassle her a bit. It got out of hand.

HEMA. Who were the others?

AKSHAY. I don't know. I was hoping to get an auto. They were hoping to catch a bus. She pissed us all off with her attitude, rude, like she owned the street – She wasn't like you, Amma.

HEMA. Me?

AKSHAY. You, you don't look into a man's eyes when you walk past him. No good woman does. She did. She looked at me. She looked at them. They wanted to teach her a lesson… I, I wanted to help her… I wanted to warn her to behave like a good woman, for her own sake. But she wouldn't listen. She started calling us names, and one thing led to another and they were on her.

Silence.

HEMA. And you were too.

Silence.

AKSHAY. A *rakshasan* was in my veins that night. My head, my heart… I felt feral, like I was inhabiting the body of a beast. I felt sleek… and powerful. I liked that. I liked who I became… A warrior… A lion. I didn't feel lonely. I didn't feel like I had no place in this world. I connected with those men… We all belonged to each other for a brief time. We were brothers-in-arms. And for the first time, there was no past… no future… Only the present… and we were kings.

Silence.

Are they going to arrest me? Are you going to let them?

Silence.

No, you won't do that. You won't let them. I am your only child. I am your world.

Silence.

HEMA. You disgust me. I disgust myself.

AKSHAY. Go on. Go sit in the shadows looking like a martyr. Remember though, it's his blood inside of me. And yours. Both of you messed me up. All my life, I've been trying to make both of you happy. If Appa was pleased, you got upset. If you were pleased, Appa broke my bones. My life has been a minefield. What choice did a boy have?

HEMA. Are you blaming me for what you did?

AKSHAY. I've wanted to come home for months. You wouldn't let me.

HEMA. You know why. This house is cursed. I wanted you far away from it.

AKSHAY. That's not the truth. You never wanted me here, with you, because I remind you too much of him. You should have let me come home. You should have let me heal here. You shouldn't have let me fend for myself in a strange city. I don't even speak their language! You wanted me away from his shadows so badly you never saw the darkness inside me, eating me up.

AKSHAY *kneels before his mother and tries to hug her, like a little boy.* HEMA *is an ice statue.*

I want to begin anew. I want to not hate myself so much. I want to be everything you want me to be. Maybe Patti is right.

HEMA. What do you mean?

AKSHAY. Maybe if I perform the ceremony, it will all stop, the *rakshasan* will go away. I have to do it, don't you see?

HEMA. May we all rot in hell.

HEMA *leaves.*

AKSHAY. Fuck you!

Scene Thirteen

AKSHAY *performs the ancestral ritual. He is bare-chested and wears a* veshti *and the sacred thread. Sacred fire has been lit. Sounds of chanting of mantras.* AKSHAY *pays his respects to his father and his dead ancestors.*

Scene Fourteen

A café in Chennai.

UMA. I've been waiting for two hours.

AKSHAY. I told you I was delayed.

UMA. 'Slightly delayed', you said. And that was an hour and a half ago. And not a single response to any of my texts or voice messages.

AKSHAY. And yet here you still are.

UMA. I've a flight to catch in an hour.

AKSHAY. More coffee?

UMA. No. We reworked *Penguin Waddle*. It's live now –

AKSHAY. Is this the menu?

UMA. Everyone is absolutely delighted with it. We nearly couldn't make it because a certain member of the team suddenly upped and vanished, but it didn't matter in the end. Everyone pitched in, everyone put in that much more.

   AKSHAY *gets up and exits with the menu.*

   Akshay.

   UMA *is left alone. She gets increasingly worked up. She drinks some more coffee. She tries to get* AKSHAY*'s attention. She checks her phone. She checks her watch.*

   AKSHAY *returns with a tray full of food.*

   Have you checked it out?

AKSHAY. I love this mango cake.

UMA. There are thirty-five thousand users already. Four-star rated. Four-point-two in fact and rising steadily.

AKSHAY. I think it's the mangoes. Chennai has the best mangoes in the country.

UMA. It's got great reviews. *Tech Today* called it a game that anyone can play, not just the men. When it went live, we went to the bar to celebrate. A different bar. We couldn't go back *there* again. David has been arrested. Do you know?

AKSHAY. No.

UMA. They're calling him one of the culprits. It's so wrong. He tried to save her.

AKSHAY. So he says.

UMA. He was your friend! He was always looking out for you!

AKSHAY. Surely you haven't flown all the way from Mumbai to tell me what I already know?

Pause.

UMA. KRS sent me here to talk to you. I believe you set your lawyers on us. KRS believes David acted in haste in firing you. KRS has had time to think and he regrets he wasn't more 'active' in the running of the company. He wishes we can all forget what happened and you can get back to being a valued colleague. So, basically, what I'm saying is, you're un-fired, and when can you join work? We're beginning work on three more projects. A racing game, a brick game and an escape –

AKSHAY. You want me back –

UMA. The company, yes.

AKSHAY. But not you? (*Beat.*) I'm sorry, I can't work in a place where my colleagues are openly hostile towards me.

Pause.

UMA. It would give me great pleasure if you rejoin work. Please.

AKSHAY (*laughs*). Patti was fucking right after all!

What's the offer?

UMA. Offer?

AKSHAY. You can't expect me to continue as if nothing has happened.

UMA. We're willing to consider the last few weeks as paid leave.

AKSHAY. Not good enough. I want a fifty-per-cent hike in basic.

UMA. Are you out of your mind?

AKSHAY. Actually, I want your job. Tell him that. Let me know what he decides. Should I order another mango cake or should I try something else?

AKSHAY *studies the menu*. UMA *studies* AKSHAY.

UMA. David came to my flat early that morning after he put the girl in the ambulance. He was violently ill. He couldn't say a word. They got the wrong man. Don't you agree? (*Silence.*) Come on, Akshay! If he did it, you did it!

AKSHAY. But I didn't do it. Also, I want a written apology from you. For slandering me and destroying my reputation.

UMA. What?

AKSHAY. And a conduct certificate attesting to my good behaviour at work and sound character.

Pause.

UMA. Ten-per-cent hike in basic and grade-two promotion. That's all we can offer. Happy now?

Pause.

AKSHAY. I should be, shouldn't I? Everything is going the way I want.

UMA. Are you though?

Silence.

I know the pressure on the boss to take you back is coming from your mother and uncle. Even now, you run behind them like a little boy when the going gets tough.

AKSHAY. I think you've missed your flight.

Scene Fifteen

1:30 a.m. RAGINI *sneaks in, when someone switches on the light. It is* AKSHAY.

RAGINI. Oh, you gave me a fright! So sorry, I lost track of time. Have Amma and Patti gone to bed?

AKSHAY. Yes.

RAGINI. My watch stopped.

AKSHAY. The same old excuse? Surely you could come up with something more original?

RAGINI (*laughs*). Nevertheless it's the truth. Why were you in pitch dark?

AKSHAY. I was playing some games. I must have fallen asleep. I'm on level twelve now. (*Pause.*) Would you like to join me?

RAGINI. Patti will really have a double coronary if she sees me not working, and with you at that!

AKSHAY. I can take care of Patti –

RAGINI. Thanks but no. People like me don't have the luxury of time. Better go and check on Patti before she starts gnawing my brain out.

AKSHAY. She's asleep. I checked.

RAGINI. You're so gullible. That woman never sleeps at night.

AKSHAY. Did you have a good time?

RAGINI. The best. We did another movie marathon today. From the first show of the day to the last.

AKSHAY. 'We'?

JAYA (*off*). Ragini! Are you back?

RAGINI (*to off*). Yes, Patti!

What did I tell you?

RAGINI *lingers by the door.*

Can you get drunk on simply being at the cinema? I'm cinema-drunk. I feel somehow, elevated, like I'm existing on a different plane now.

AKSHAY. What films did you see?

RAGINI. Oh, the films were rubbish. But it's the whole ambience, the feeling of community. I met this director at the second movie. We were the only five people there. But here's the incredible thing. This director offered me a role in his next film.

AKSHAY. As what?

RAGINI. As a 'village belle'. (*Pause*.) Here's where you say, (*With some exaggeration*.) 'Really?' or 'How amazing for you!'

Pause.

AKSHAY. What is your… story arc?

RAGINI. What is that?

AKSHAY. Your character. What does she do? Where does she go?

RAGINI. No idea. What does a village belle do? She hangs out with the chaste heroine, I guess.

AKSHAY. You don't know –

RAGINI. No.

AKSHAY. You didn't ask.

RAGINI. No. He gave me his card. See?

AKSHAY. Never heard of him.

RAGINI. He's someone alright. Not big, but not obscure either. Up-and-coming, hotshot director and he saw me and said, 'You have an expressive face. I'd like to use you in my film.'

JAYA (*off*). Ragini!

RAGINI (*to* JAYA, *off*). Yes Patti?

JAYA. My water jug is empty.

RAGINI. Yes, Patti!

AKSHAY. You said 'no', of course.

RAGINI. 'Of course'?

AKSHAY. It's an exploitative profession. It's not for girls like you.

RAGINI. I said I'll think about it. Won't do to sound overeager, no? There are just three scenes and he was looking for the right girl. He said he'd pay me fifty thousand rupees.

Pause.

AKSHAY. He wants to sleep with you.

RAGINI. What a horrible thing to say!

AKSHAY. I know the way men's minds work. You aren't going to take it up, are you?

RAGINI *shrugs*. *Pause*.

Who will take care of Patti when you're gone?

RAGINI. The agency will send a replacement. Look, I'm not that important here. What I'm doing here, anyone can do. Besides, Patti would be thrilled with me gone.

AKSHAY. It looks like you've made up your mind.

Just want you to know, if you've been hearing stories about this house…

RAGINI. I have not.

AKSHAY. They're all false.

RAGINI. Okay.

Silence.

AKSHAY. I'll give you the money.

RAGINI. What?

JAYA (*off*). Girl, my throat is parched!

AKSHAY. I understand the money is tempting.

RAGINI. Thanks, but I cannot accept it. I have to go to Patti.

AKSHAY. I was waiting up for you –

RAGINI. You shouldn't have. It's sweet, but don't do that.

AKSHAY. I kept thinking of you the whole day –

RAGINI. You shouldn't do that. You shouldn't think about me, you certainly shouldn't say that you do. It sends the wrong message. I mean, you've a tendency not to think things through when you say stuff like this.

AKSHAY. I mean it.

JAYA (*off*). Girl! What will it take to get some water in this house? I am dying!

AKSHAY. You understand me like no one else does.

RAGINI. I don't. You're making no sense. (*Laughs.*) See, I don't understand you at all.

Ping of a message. RAGINI *checks it.*

AKSHAY. Who is it from?

RAGINI. A friend.

AKSHAY. A boyfriend?

Beat.

RAGINI. Yes.

You are blocking my path.

AKSHAY. Does your family know? Do they approve of your relationship? Do they care that your reputation is being sullied?

RAGINI (*yells*). Patti! Are you still awake?

JAYA. I am now!

RAGINI (*yells*). Do you want water?

JAYA. Do you have dementia or what? Water, girl! Is that too much to ask for in this house?

AKSHAY. Look, I'm sorry. It's come out the wrong way. I apologise.

RAGINI. It's fine.

AKSHAY. Are we friends again?

RAGINI. Yes, of course.

Please, I have to go.

HEMA *enters*.

HEMA. What's with all the yelling? There are people trying to sleep.

She clocks RAGINI *and* AKSHAY.

You've returned finally. You couldn't have called to let me know you'd be late? It's highly irresponsible of you. I expected better.

JAYA (*off*). Ragini! Have you gone to a bloody river to fetch water or what?

HEMA. Why are you hanging around? Go and give it!

RAGINI (*to* JAYA, *off*). Coming, Patti!

RAGINI *exits*.

HEMA. What happened back here?

AKSHAY. Nothing. (*Pause.*) What do you think happened?

Silence.

HEMA. I'm going to stay here. I'm going to watch some TV, if you don't mind.

HEMA *switches on the TV. She prepares to keep vigil on the couch.* AKSHAY *leaves.*

Scene Sixteen

Two days later. JAYA*'s room.*

HEMA. Are you wearing your diaper?

JAYA. Yes. Who'll look after me now? You who can't breathe the same air as me for five minutes?

HEMA. No, obviously not. We'll kill each other. I've asked the agency to send someone else. Someone older. Someone old.

JAYA. You always go out of your way to make me miserable.

HEMA. Do you think I want to let her go? She certainly knows how to handle you. How many nurses I had to change until she came along? I've lost count.

JAYA. Don't think I didn't notice you didn't say a word to stop her.

HEMA. If she wants to go, we have to let her.

JAYA. Can't she wait for a few weeks? The muddy water is just settling. Things are just beginning to look bright and clear.

HEMA. Are they?

JAYA. Everything is going to be alright. He is a good boy. Like Lord Rama. You find him a Sita and he'll be better than alright.

HEMA. You once said I was Jagan's Sita and everything would be alright.

JAYA. If we persist with our faithfulness, like Sita did, we will be rewarded.

HEMA. How? She had to walk through fire to prove her chastity. She did that, but did she live happily ever after? No. Because Rama overheard some stupid gossip about her and decided to banish her, his pregnant queen, from his kingdom. So you tell me, where the hell is her reward? Where the hell is mine?

JAYA. Her children were her reward. Your son is yours. (*Pause. Re: outside the window.*) What does that Gopi want now?

HEMA *goes to the window. She puts on a smile and waves to an unseen* GOPI.

HEMA. Nothing. He's just being friendly. The room looks brighter since the tree went, doesn't it?

JAYA. It's too bright. It gives me a migraine.

AKSHAY *enters.*

AKSHAY. What does?

Pause.

JAYA. The room. The Sun God is galloping on his seven horses straight into this room. I need sunglasses inside.

AKSHAY. I've brought you a few things to read.

JAYA. Hema, look! A present for me!

AKSHAY. *Amar Chitra Katha.* Mythological comics.

JAYA. Oh thank you, *kanna.* You remembered that I love them. I've bought so many of them for you when you were a child –

AKSHAY. And now I'm buying them for you!

And something for you.

AKSHAY *gives* HEMA *a sari.*

Do you remember you had one like this years ago when you took me to the zoo? It was the happiest time of my childhood. Just the two of us and those white tigers.

HEMA. This is… sweet.

AKSHAY. I want nothing but the best for my favourite girls.

JAYA (*to* HEMA). See? Already we are getting blessed. (*To* AKSHAY.) Don't you feel it? Your father is happy with you.

AKSHAY. Did the crow tell you that?

JAYA *laughs*.

JAYA. Now all you have to do is work hard and leave the rest to your karma. Your father is taking care of you now.

AKSHAY. I don't know about Appa, but Amma certainly is. Aren't you?

JAYA. Of course she would. A mother always looks after her son.

Is that fellow still staring at us?

AKSHAY. Who is?

JAYA. Dr Buffoon.

HEMA *looks out the window*.

HEMA. No, ma.

JAYA. He's spying on me. His head is turned our way.

HEMA. Can't he look in our direction at all? Is that a criminal offence?

AKSHAY. I'll get back to work and you girls get back to… squabbling.

AKSHAY *laughs. He exits. Sound of the door being bolted.* JAYA *has heard it.* HEMA *hasn't.*

HEMA. He's probably on the phone, hands-free, silly woman. Stop being so paranoid. There. He's gone back inside.

Are you sure you're wearing a diaper? It's stinking in here.

JAYA. Where are you going?

HEMA. I'm going to ask Ragini to clean the room and wash your sheets before she leaves. Then I've to cook. You're the one who keeps yelling to all and sundry that I'm starving you.

JAYA. Hema, come sit. Just for a few minutes. Please.

When I got married, my mother-in-law told me this story.

HEMA. No no no, you're not going to trick me into listening to one more of your –

JAYA. No, this one is special. You're going to love it! Don't go yet. We're talking like old friends. I like it. Stay.

Pause.

HEMA. Two minutes. That's all.

JAYA. Long time ago, there was this man who wanted his wife to be with him all the time. So he transformed her into water and carried her in a small vessel, wherever he went.

HEMA. A portable wife!

JAYA. His wife loved being water. It made her feel free. She loved it so much she wanted to become a river and travel to new lands. But the husband wouldn't allow it. One day, when he was asleep, Lord Ganesha happened to pass that way. He saw the vessel with water in it. He saw the woman in the vessel. He took the form of a crow and pecked at the vessel just hard enough for it to tilt and the water to spill into the ground. For the first time in her life, the woman was free, free to do anything she wanted. So she turned into a mighty river and flowed away, far far away from her husband. She still flows today as the mighty river Cauvery.

HEMA. That's… nice. What exactly are you trying to say?

A black feather falls on JAYA*'s bed.*

JAYA. All the times you wanted to run away from him, I should have let you. I shouldn't have made you come back.

HEMA. Yes. You shouldn't have used my boy as a weapon.

JAYA. Sometimes we do things for the sake of one's family. I didn't want to lose my son. You didn't want to lose yours.

HEMA. All water under the bridge now.

JAYA. Is it really? I desperately want it to be so.

A moment of connection between the two women.

HEMA. Let me see if Ragini has finished packing up her things.

JAYA. Hema?

JAYA *struggles to articulate. Silence.*

Can you put on some music?

HEMA. Now you want to listen, huh?

You look pale. Have you had all your meds today?

JAYA. Yes yes.

HEMA. I should remember to ask Ragini for your medicine schedule.

HEMA *feels* JAYA's *skin.*

You're clammy. Should I call Dr Gopi?

JAYA. No! No doctor! I'm sure. I want to listen to music. That's all. Please.

HEMA. Which one? –

JAYA. Anything.

HEMA. There's MS's Meera Bhajans. There's Bombay Jayshree, Gayathri Mantra – what are you in the mood for?

JAYA. Just put something on.

HEMA *puts on* JAYA's *CD from Scene One.*

Hema. Please sit down.

HEMA. Just relax, okay? Take deep breaths. Let me go get Ragini. She'll know what to do.

JAYA *grabs* HEMA's *hand.*

JAYA. No, just sit with me. I'll be alright.

HEMA *feels* JAYA's *forehead.*

HEMA. You are scaring me.

JAYA. Just stay. I just want to spend some time with my daughter.

HEMA. That's a change. From bitch to daughter!

JAYA. I had to adapt, I had to survive for the sake of my child. Just as you had to for yours.

They listen. Another black feather falls. Only JAYA *notices them.*

Louder please.

HEMA. This is an old building. You'll bring the roof down!

Fine.

HEMA *increases the volume. They listen for a bit. Then* HEMA *reduces the volume.*

Our eardrums are not young any more.

They listen for a bit.

I hate your music. You used to put it on constantly before. When Jagan was alive. That was what I heard when Jagan got into a mood.

More black feathers fall.

I'm going to put on something else. This is giving me too many bad memories.

JAYA. No! Leave it be!

HEMA. How about Western classical for a change? There's one here.

JAYA. No! Leave the player alone.

HEMA *stops the CD player.*

HEMA. Something else. I can't bear to hear –

A bloodcurdling scream of a woman is heard offstage. HEMA *goes to the door. It's locked. She bangs on the door.*

Ragini!

Akshay! Open the door!

Akshay! Don't do anything stupid!

RAGINI*'s voice is muffled.* HEMA p*icks up her mobile phone and calls. We can hear a phone ring offstage. Then the sound of the phone crashing against the wall offstage. Then silence.*

The feathers fall.

JAYA. Please… put on the music.

In shock, HEMA *turns up the music. They sit, motionless.*

What choice do we have? I thought I could change, we could all change…

HEMA *stares at* JAYA.

You're right. It's this house. It's cursed.

HEMA. The house.

JAYA. Or maybe it's the blood that's cursed. Jagan's, Akshay's.

HEMA. All I ever wanted was for him to be a good man.

JAYA. Me also. For my boy. We made mistakes but our intentions were noble.

GOPI *appears outside the window.*

GOPI (*over the music*). Can you lower the noise please? I'm trying to enjoy birdless silence.

HEMA *gets up and goes to the window.*

JAYA (*to* HEMA). Don't do it. Our reputation… Our family… Let it go. Just close your eyes and listen to the music. Forget everything.

You go to him, you'll lose your son forever. You can't bear that, Hema.

GOPI (*over the music*). Is everything okay?

JAYA. We're alright. We're fine. You can leave.

RAGINI*'s cry for help is heard clearly now.*

If that's our fate, then that's our fate.

GOPI. Hema –

HEMA. It is on me, he said. It's all on me. He will keep doing it and it will all be on me.

GOPI. What is going on?

JAYA. Nothing is going on. We're fine. We're having an argument, that's all. It's normal, between mother and daughter. Hema, ask him to leave!

GOPI. Who is screaming? Can't you hear it?

JAYA. I hear nothing.

GOPI *turns to leave*. HEMA *makes a decision*.

HEMA. Gopi *na*! Wait! Don't go!

We are not alright. We are locked in.

JAYA. No, Hema!

HEMA. The woman… help her! It's my son.

GOPI *realises that something dire is happening. He yells 'Police, Police!' as he rushes (to the road) to gather people. Commotion. Noises of many people running towards the house. People breaking down a door. The room is filled with feathers. The room turns red. Cawing of many crows. Blackout.*

The End.

www.nickhernbooks.co.uk

facebook.com/nickhernbooks

twitter.com/nickhernbooks